T0332383

A UNIVOCAL BOOK

DREW BURK, CONSULTING EDITOR

Univocal Publishing was founded by Jason Wagner and Drew Burk as an independent publishing house specializing in artisanal editions and translations of texts spanning the areas of cultural theory, media archeology, continental philosophy, aesthetics, anthropology, and more. In May 2017, Univocal ceased operations as an independent publishing house and became a series with its publishing partner, the University of Minnesota Press.

UNIVOCAL AUTHORS INCLUDE:

Miguel Abensour	Évelyne Grossman	Jacques Rancière
Judith Balso	Félix Guattari	Lionel Ruffel
Jean Baudrillard	Olivier Haralambon	Felwine Sarr
Philippe Beck	David Lapoujade	Michel Serres
Simon Critchley	François Laruelle	Gilbert Simondon
Fernand Deligny	David Link	Étienne Souriau
Jacques Derrida	Sylvère Lotringer	Isabelle Stengers
Vinciane Despret	Jean Malaurie	Sylvain Tesson
Georges Didi-Huberman	Michael Marder	Eugene Thacker
Jean Epstein	Serge Margel	Antoine Volodine
Vilém Flusser	Quentin Meillassoux	Elisabeth von Samsonow
Barbara Glowczewski	Friedrich Nietzsche	Siegfried Zielinski
	Peter Pál Pelbart	

WORLDS BUILT
TO FALL APART

A Univocal Book

DAVID LAPOUJADE

WORLDS BUILT TO FALL APART

VERSIONS OF PHILIP K. DICK

TRANSLATED BY ERIK BERANEK

UNIVERSITY OF MINNESOTA PRESS

MINNEAPOLIS / LONDON

Originally published in French as *L'Altération des mondes:*
Versions de Philip K. Dick; copyright 2021 by Les Éditions de Minuit.

Translation copyright 2024 by the Regents of the University of Minnesota

Published by the University of Minnesota Press

111 Third Avenue South, Suite 290

Minneapolis, MN 55401-2520

http://www.upress.umn.edu

ISBN 978-1-5179-1461-5 (pb)

A Cataloging-in-Publication record for this book is available from the Library of Congress.

Printed in the United States of America on acid-free paper

The University of Minnesota is an equal-opportunity educator and employer.

33 32 31 30 29 28 27 26 25 24   10 9 8 7 6 5 4 3 2 1

CONTENTS

TRANSLATOR'S PREFACE

ERIK BERANEK

> Heaven knows what we mean by reality. Telephone, tinned meat, Charlie
> Chaplin, water-taps, and World-Salvation, presumably. Some insisting on
> the plumbing, and some on saving the world: these being the two great
> American specialties.
>
> D. H. LAWRENCE, *STUDIES IN CLASSIC AMERICAN LITERATURE*

This book can be read in a variety of ways. First and foremost, it should
be read as a close engagement with the works of Philip K. Dick, and as
such, it will appeal to fans of Dick's works and to readers of science
fiction more generally. One of the book's key merits is the great quan-
tity of material *by* Dick with which David Lapoujade works: thirty-three
novels and forty-six stories, as well as several important essays and
interviews from throughout Dick's career and a number of discussions
revolving around *The Exegesis*. By situating these works in conversation with a wide array of Dick's influences—from Carl Jung and the *I
Ching* to the contributions to cybernetic theory of Norbert Weiner and
Gregory Bateson and the general semantics of Alfred Korzybski—
Lapoujade gives a rich portrait of Dick's unique intellectual world. That

said, this book also represents a fascinating step in the development of Lapoujade's own philosophical thought, and so for the benefit of any readers less familiar with Lapoujade than with Dick himself, I would like to offer a few remarks situating the book in terms of Lapoujade's philosophy.

For the past fifteen years, David Lapoujade has been publishing a remarkable series of philosophical and critical studies, all but one of which have already been translated into English. After editing two volumes of essays by Gilles Deleuze (*Desert Islands* and *Two Regimes of Madness*—he also later edited Deleuze's *Letters and Other Texts*), he wrote a striking introduction to the empiricism and pragmatism of William James; an exploration of relations as they function in the works of both William and Henry James; a penetrating study of several crucial though often overlooked aspects of Henri Bergson's philosophy; a brilliant rethinking of Deleuze's oeuvre as an encyclopedia of aberrant movements; and an introduction to Étienne Souriau's philosophy of modes of existence.

Several things clearly hold the works of this series together. For one thing, there is the presence of Deleuze, with whom Lapoujade studied and whose work represents a significant encounter in the development of his thought. Readers of Deleuze will recognize Bergson and William and Henry James as important figures in the fabric of Deleuze's thought, and the recent revival of interest in Souriau can be traced in part to a reference to his *L'Instauration Philosophique* in Deleuze and Guattari's *What Is Philosophy?* What's more, there is a certain stylistic similarity between these works and Deleuze's early studies in the history of philosophy. It appears as though Lapoujade has been working to constitute a canon of philosophical forebears, one that overlaps at times with Deleuze's own alternative history of philosophy, to be sure, yet that takes up the impetus of this Deleuzian gesture in its own way and for its own ends. James the "radical empiricist," Bergson the "superior empiricist," Deleuze the "transcendental empiricist," and Souriau the existential pluralist—it seems clear that Lapoujade's works have been exploring a still minor tradition of rethinking empiricism and pragmatism and inviting us to take up the redistribution of philosophical problems that it has led to.

But where does Philip K. Dick fit into all of this? While it is true that Deleuze said that a book of philosophy should be "in part a kind of science fiction," references to science fiction itself are quite rare in his work, and he never made a science fiction author the subject of a study. Whereas Lapoujade frequently incorporates literary references into his philosophical reflections—there is Henry James, of course, but countless other literary references are found throughout his works—up to this point in his writing, there has never been any indication that science fiction would emerge as a topic of interest. Moreover, generally speaking, doesn't science fiction remain something of an outlier genre, still deemed by some to be unworthy of "serious study"? And, within this already marginalized realm, doesn't Dick himself occupy a somewhat peripheral and extravagant place? Undoubtedly, he remains one of the most influential science fiction authors, and yet, despite his famed penchant for building his stories around epistemological problems, don't the drugs, the mysticism, and the endless paranoia make it somewhat difficult to reconcile his writings with philosophical theory?

On the other hand, there is a way in which this book can be read as a direct development of the last chapter of Lapoujade's previous book on Souriau. That book—*The Lesser Existences: Étienne Souriau, an Aesthetics for the Virtual*—functions effectively as an introduction to Souriau's thought. Unlike William James, Bergson, and Deleuze, whose works are already entrenched in fairly established interpretations, Souriau remains relatively unknown even in France. In the former case, when writing on James, Bergson, or Deleuze, Lapoujade was able to use his studies to displace their thought from the usual interpretations and to establish new connections. In the case of Souriau, however, Lapoujade presents *The Lesser Existences* as a more straightforward introduction to the main features of Souriau's thought, focusing on identifying a main line of questioning and developing a reading of Souriau's major concepts on that basis. And yet, even under the guise of a more straightforward approach, Lapoujade still gives it a particular twist of his own.

As with the patchwork world of William James's pluralistic universe, Souriau's philosophy aims to shift the emphasis from a single, preexisting reality, within which everything that exists would be found, to an interrogation into the various ways in which different kinds of existences do in fact exist and exist as distinct manners of existing. For Souriau, a stone exists, a person exists, and a tree exists, but a forest exists in a manner all its own, separate from the individual trees; likewise, a fictional character like Don Quixote, the idea of a nation, and the unmade film to which an already written screenplay refers all have their distinct modes of existence. Particularly important within Souriau's analysis of these different modes are virtual existences, which is to say incomplete existences or existences in the making that seem to call for an intensification and development of their own reality. Souriau refuses to make these existences dependent on the mind that would be the agent of their completion, looking at them rather as existences that make a claim on their own future development. As a result, he is able to push away from the traditional primacy of the already fully constituted to show a picture in which the world remains something in the making, one in which existences can exist with a greater or lesser reality and must affirm their own rights to exist.

In the final chapter of the book, Lapoujade pushes Souriau's analysis one step further, making explicit a political dimension already inherent in the aesthetic and metaphysical problems that Souriau raises. Lapoujade turns his attention to those existences that find themselves dispossessed of their reality; that is, those beings that find themselves to have *less reality* than others who control what has been determined as *most real*. If existences need to make a claim on their own reality and right to exist, what happens when an existence is prevented from doing so by other forces within its world and is therefore stripped and dispossessed of the very reality to which it makes its claim? Through discussions of a wide variety of artists—from writers like Kafka and Beckett to visual artists like Agnes Martin and Robert Rauschenberg to video artists like Bill Viola and Nam June Paik—we come to see a picture of twentieth-century art as striving to give a sensible presence to the particular types of limits to which these dispossessed existences are pushed in their attempt to grapple with a reality that has been taken from them.

Dick could easily have been featured in that chapter. It almost seems as if Lapoujade could have begun his engagement with Dick there, but then realized the extent to which his work would require a discussion entirely its own. For Dick, any preexisting faith in the world is almost always taken away from his characters, whether through implanted memories, drugs, psychosis, or thoughts beamed into the mind by a government agency or extraterrestrial satellite. There is always something preventing the characters from taking the reality of their world for granted; there is always a combat going on between two realities in struggle.

Following the work of *The Lesser Existences*, Lapoujade here shows how the worlds that Dick constructs are always on the point of collapsing, precisely because they are worlds whose appearances are determined by a clash of multiple minds vying for control. What's more, the stories are often told from the perspective of a perfectly unremarkable character: an average person whose rather average problems have little to do with the fate of humanity yet become bound up with some larger force or confrontation. In Lapoujade's hands, the drugs, the psychosis, and the fantastic, paranormal occurrences that are commonplace in Dick's writings all result from the constancy of this struggle in which certain minds exert an influence or control over the appearances of the world that other minds are forced to live in. This is a problem that, for Dick, is theoretical, theological, and psychiatric but that also relates to the invasion of advertising images and disposable luxuries in the public sphere, the proliferation of new technologies in everyday life, and the rapid development of a new service-based society with its attendant new forms of surveillance and control. Insofar as Dick's work dramatizes this type of *very real* struggle, giving us a way to understand a form of dispossession that makes certain that *really real* beings exist in a manner that is *less real* than certain others, we might say that he is something of a "physician of civilization," a term of Nietzschean provenance that Lapoujade uses to describe Bergson in the third chapter of *Powers of Time*. To be sure, the present book should be read as a critical essay, but also as a clinical one.

There is another connection with Lapoujade's work on Bergson worth mentioning here. For Bergson, the intellect becomes overdeveloped to the point of dissolving our relation to ourselves, to society, and to the world. Lapoujade shows how first obedience, then fabulation, and then ultimately mysticism and creative emotion create ways of maintaining our attachment to life in the face of this dissolution and are for Bergson constitutive of humans' social and historical existence. In Dick, then, the extreme overdevelopment of the intellect—or, as he will put it, of the brain's "digital" left hemisphere—to the point of androidization, is a constant and central theme that threatens to overwhelm and even eliminate the empathetic, sympathetic relations of the right hemisphere. Lapoujade understands this latter kind of relation in a manner that hearkens back to the notion of sympathy that he analyzes in his discussion of Bergsonian intuition in *Powers of Time*. In Dick's work, the left brain and the intellect are represented by figures like the android and the engineer, while the intuitive, sympathetic right brain tends to be represented by the handyman, the tinkerer, or the bricoleur, a figure famously developed in Lévi-Strauss's *La pensée sauvage*, which Lapoujade discusses at length in the final chapter of this book. If Dick is, in fact, a physician of civilization, it is certainly due to the vision and symptomology of contemporary society that his works present, but also to his promotion of the figure of the bricoleur as the person most suited to the *time after*, the person who mends and patches together fragments of a world, not with the aim of reconstructing the world of violence and exclusion that came before but in the service of an intuitive relationship to the world that forges connections of sympathy and empathy, piecing it back together in a manner completely otherwise.

Without a doubt, much remains to be said about these connections back to Lapoujade's work on Souriau and Bergson, and the list of connections could certainly be expanded to include his other books as well. But rather than overdetermine things, I would prefer simply to welcome the reader into this introduction to a multiplicity of "versions" of Philip K. Dick, displaced from any cartoonish notion one might have of him and brought in on his own terms as a thinker of radical empiricism. While reading this book, perhaps you'll start to see his works as spiritual siblings of Deleuze and Guattari's *Anti-Oedipus*, or maybe you'll be tempted to imagine *The Exegesis* as a case study in James's *The Varieties of Religious Experience*, or hear Horselover Fat as an added interlocutor in Hume's *Dialogues Concerning Natural Religion*. Be that as it may, I hope that *Worlds Built to Fall Apart: Versions of Philip K. Dick* will lead you back to the novels and stories of Philip K. Dick, reading them to enjoy them, but also with a renewed understanding of the ways in which certain seemingly extravagant features of Dick's worlds—the mind-altering drugs, the madness, the acute experiences of religious delirium—come together with the resources of science fiction as a means of diagnosing a world that has come unhinged.

Each translation entails challenges all its own, though these often remain invisible in the finished text. In the present case, perhaps the most difficult part of my work was returning the many passages from Dick's works, essays, and interviews, which the author cited in their French translations, back into English. Doing so required many hours of research and veritable mountains of books, and I am thankful to the librarians at the Firestone Library and the Van Pelt Library for the important part they played in making that happen. I would also like to thank Samuel Martin, my good friend and coeditor at *Hopscotch Translation*, whose input has been invaluable throughout the process. Above all others, I am endlessly grateful to Kelsey Borrowman, without whom none of this would have been possible. I feel very lucky that "the world she wanted" overlaps so nicely with my own.

WORLDS BUILT TO FALL APART

INTRODUCTION

ON DELIRIUM

I'm surprised at you [. . .]. Really, I am. You sound like a college sophomore.
Solipsism—skepticism. Bishop Berkeley, all that ultimate-reality stuff.

PHILIP K. DICK, *THE MAN WHO JAPED*

SF thinks with worlds.[1] Creating new worlds with different physical
laws, different conditions for life, different life forms, and different political organizations; creating parallel worlds and inventing passages
between them; multiplying worlds—such is the essential occupation
of SF. The war of the worlds, the best or worst of all worlds, and the
ways the world comes to an end are its recurring themes. Sometimes
these worlds belong to distant galaxies, sometimes they are parallel
worlds accessed through secret portals or breaches in our own world,
and sometimes they take shape following the destruction of the human
world. The only condition is that these worlds be *other*—or, when we
are dealing with our own world, that it has been rendered sufficiently
unrecognizable to have become other. We might even say that SF oc-
cupies itself with destroying worlds. The total wars, cataclysms, alien
invasions, fatal viruses, apocalypses, and other kinds of end-of-the-

world we find in SF are countless. There are numerous possibilities, but in each case it is a question of thinking in terms of worlds.

The trade-off is that SF struggles to create singular characters like those produced by classical literature. There is no Achilles, Lancelot, or Mrs. Dalloway in SF. Its characters are often ordinary individuals, stereotypes or prototypes that are only minimally individual, because they are primarily there to make us see the way a world functions or comes apart.[2] Their value lies in their being indicative samples. At the limit, the character himself doesn't even matter, as long as he makes you understand the laws that are obeyed by the world he is confronted with. The characters are never as important as the worlds in which they live. Given the conditions of some world or other, how do the characters adapt? Given a group of characters, what strange worlds are they confronted with? Such are the two principal questions that animate the stories of SF. One way or another, the characters are always secondary with respect to the world in which they are immersed or from which they are seeking to escape.

It will be objected that the truly distinctive trait of SF is its recourse to "science," which is why we speak fittingly of science fiction.[3] But here, too, science—and technology—are only means (now inherent to the genre) of propelling us toward distant worlds or of introducing us into a technologically advanced, future world. Perhaps recourse to "science" is what makes SF stand out, but it is nevertheless not what defines it. To speak like Aristotle, science and technology are properties of SF, but they do not define it.[4] However important they may be for the genre, they remain subordinate to the invention and composition of other worlds.

This also explains why SF borrows from other forms of thought that conceive or imagine other worlds, such as metaphysics, mythology, and religion. Instead of a scientific dream, doesn't each SF author really harbor a mythological, metaphysical, or religious dream, which is expressed through the creation of these other worlds? It is because they conceive of new worlds that Cyrano de Bergerac, Fontenelle, and Leibniz have been seen as precursors to SF. In philosophy, it is certainly Leibniz who has gone farthest along this path, because, for him, everything is thought in terms of worlds, and because the real world is always only one world among an infinity of other possible worlds.[5]

In addition, the way in which SF is frequently invoked today with regard to technological progress, the devastation of the Earth, and utopian or dystopian visions also bears witness to a thinking with worlds, to "world effects" provoked by flows of information. It could be said that the horizon of each piece of information is now the viability, survival, organization, and destruction of our world, and, internal to that, the relations between the various human, animal, vegetable, and mineral worlds, inasmuch as they compose or decompose the unity and variety of this world. Information no longer bears upon isolated parts of the world without concerning the state of the world in general and its insurmountable limits. It is no longer the case that each event is connected to the destiny of the world by one or a thousand threads; now, the destiny of the world hangs on the thread of each piece of information.

That is why information is tending to disappear, being replaced instead by *alerts*. The informer becomes a transmitter, an alert vector in a permanent and generalized system of alerts that is tied to the political, economic, social, and ecological state of the world, taken in its entirety. And the information itself is always more alarming, always more terrifying, and supported by data concerning the ongoing destruction of the world. Isn't that inevitable when the viability of the world—and of the multiple worlds composing it and giving it its consistency—is everywhere under threat? We aren't informed about parts of the world anymore but are on permanent alert about the general state of the world. The effect is debilitating. All the scenarios, all the simulations and hypotheses that result, whether catastrophic or not, force us to think in terms of worlds, to "globalize" even the most minute data. And that is where the junction between the actual world and SF occurs, independently of the fictional stories, as if the information concerning the present state of the world were nothing but a succession of stories anticipating its future state.

Every author no doubt has a manner all his own of creating worlds; but, if there was ever an author who was fully aware of the necessity of doing so, it was Philip K. Dick. "It is my job to create universes, as the basis for one novel after another. And I have to build them in such a way that they do not fall apart two days later. Or at least that is what my editors hope." And he immediately adds: "However, I will reveal a secret to you: I like to build universes that *do* fall apart. I like to see them come unglued, and I like to see how the characters in the novels cope with this problem. I have a secret love of chaos. There should be more of it."[6] Dick certainly responds to SF's imperative to create worlds, but his worlds have the peculiarity of falling apart extraordinarily quickly, as if they didn't have a solid enough foundation to remain standing on their own, or as if they were lacking in reality.

His worlds are unstable, susceptible to being distorted and over-turned by the events that penetrate them and dissipate their reality. That, for instance, is what an employee discovers one day when he leaves for work earlier than usual and suddenly sees the world around him disintegrate into dust. "A section of the building fell away. It rained down, a torrent of particles. Like sand."[7] Once at work, he learns that a team of technicians, having been alerted by a local desynchroniza-tion problem, had suspended the reality of a part of the world in order to execute a readjustment. Or, in the short story "Exhibit Piece," an em-ployee of the Archives, who is admiring a meticulous reconstruction of the twentieth century, finds himself so completely transported into the scene that he ends up asking himself if the actual world (we are in the twenty-second century) might not itself, after all, be a reconstruction. "Good God, Grunberg. You realize this may be nothing but an *exhibit*? You and everybody else—maybe you're not real. Just pieces of this ex-hibit" (S3, 194).

Or there is the novel *Time Out of Joint*, whose main character, a quiet denizen of a small town, sees the world around him undergo strange alterations. A soft-drink stand vanishes into thin air before his eyes, replaced by a small slip of paper with the words "SOFT-DRINK STAND" printed on it in block letters. As the phenomenon repeats itself, he de-cides to lead an inquiry into the reality of the world. How to interpret these slips of paper that resemble something like stage directions? Could someone be trying to deceive him? Maybe he has gone mad or is even in the center of a vast conspiracy of mass manipulation? To find out, he tries to flee the town, but "they" won't let him. Why? "They've gone to a great deal of trouble to construct a sham world around me to keep me pacified. Buildings, cars, an entire town. Natural-looking, but completely unreal" (*Time Out of Joint*, 156). Is the hypothesis of the archivist in "Exhibit Piece" correct? Is the entire town an exhibit model on the human scale?

This is a recurring problem in Dick's worlds. We don't know to what extent these worlds are real or not, or whether they will reveal themselves to be as illusory as an amusement park like Disneyland. It will be said that Dick's ambition is not to construct worlds, but to show that all worlds, including the "real" world, are artificial, sometimes being mere artifacts and sometimes being collective hallucinations, political manipulations, or psychotic deliria.[8] This accords with the many statements in which Dick affirms that all his books revolve around a single problem: what is reality?[9] What is real? Many commentators have taken up this question and made it the guiding thread of his work, thereby giving it an ontological or metaphysical dimension. But this does not explain what makes his worlds so fragile and changeable. Why is it that his worlds fall apart so quickly?

It is because behind this general problem there lurks a more profound one: that of *delirium*. For Dick, to be delirious is not just to create or exude a world, but also to be completely convinced that that world is the real world. No other SF author presents as many delirious characters, constantly threatened by or suffering from madness. His universe is populated with psychotics, schizos, paranoids, neurotics, etc., but also with mental health specialists, psychiatrists, psychoanalysts, and paranormal healers. And, at one point or another, they all come up against the question of delirium: doctor, am I getting delirious or is the world going haywire? For instance, the archivist in the twenty-second century decides to consult a psychiatrist. "Look, Grunberg.

Either this is an exhibit on R level of the History Agency, or I'm a middle-class businessman with an escape fantasy. Right now I can't decide which" (S3, 196). This isn't only the case for the characters who are mad, but also for those taking drugs and medications, for those whose memories have been tampered with, and for those whose brains are being controlled by extraterrestrial beings or a virus. With nuclear wars, irradiated nature itself begins to grow delirious; it makes bodies delirious, as can be seen in the aberrant mutations of the surviving species, like the "symbiotics" of *Dr. Bloodmoney*, "several people fused together at some part of their anatomy, sharing common organs," one pancreas for six people (*Dr. Bloodmoney*, 328). Nothing escapes the power of delirium.

If we want to retain the traditional definition of SF as an exploration of future possibilities, then these possibilities need to be delirious. "The SF writer sees not just possibilities but *wild* possibilities. It's not just 'What if . . .' It's '*My God; what if. . . .*'"[10] With this simple description, Dick gives us one of the most profound aspects of his oeuvre. For him, it isn't just a question of being imaginative, of inventing new worlds with new laws of physics, bizarre biological environments, and utopian political systems. Inventions of these sorts certainly feature in Dick's work, but they aren't essential. If the possibilities are to be "delirious," they must refer back to an underlying madness, to a real danger that threatens, at each moment, to send us toppling over the brink into madness. It is therefore less a question of freeing ourselves from the real world in order to imagine new possible worlds than of descending into the depths of the real in order to figure out which new deliria are at work there. Compared to earlier classics, Dick is much closer to Cervantes and the deliria of Don Quixote or to the Maupassant of "The Horla," than to Cyrano de Bergerac's *A Voyage to the Moon* or to the novels of Jules Verne. The powers of delirium are of a much more disquieting nature than the possibilities of the imagination, because they make the very notion of reality stagger and lurch.

Without a doubt, the strangeness of the worlds found in SF tends to disorient its characters, to confront them with irrational situations that seem destined to make them lose their minds. SF needs this irrationality as one of its essential components, even if everything is explained in the end and the hero regains his reason. In Dick's work, however, madness insinuates itself everywhere, affects everyone, and is just as often produced by extraterrestrials and drugs as it is by the social order, marriage, and political authorities. Even everyday objects go on the fritz and stop behaving the way they should. A coffee machine no longer offers coffee, producing little cups of soap instead. A door refuses to open, declaring: "The paths of glory lead but to the grave."[11] Computers grow paranoid or appear to be psychotic. "We have here a sick, deranged piece of electronic junk. We were right. Thank God we caught it in time. It's psychotic. Cosmic, schizophrenic delusions of the reality of archetypes. Good grief, the machine regards itself as an instrument of God!"[12] Many people believe that they get Dick's work when they make him the author *par excellence* of an ontological or metaphysical interrogation ("what is reality?"), but, for him, the question is primarily of a *clinical* order. The ontological and metaphysical dimensions are not merely flights of imagination but point to questions relating to mental health and the dangers of madness.

We can see why he became an SF author, though he also wrote conventional, "realist" novels (which also feature delirious characters). Maybe the realism of the conventional novel deprived delirium of its force. If you accept the assumption that there only exists one "real" world, then deliria will inevitably be treated as secondary realities that are relative, pathological, and, in short, "subjective." But if, on the other hand, you go back to the traditional definition of SF as an exploration of possible worlds, you no longer need to grant any primacy whatsoever to the "real" world, even if the majority of SF authors do ultimately preserve a form of realism that accords with their own world. The advantage of SF, for Dick, is that the real world is only ever one world of many, and not always the most "real" among them.

What does the force of delirium consist in? We could certainly think of the delirious person as being cut off from communal reality, enclosed in "his" world with his hallucinations, his erroneous judgments, and his extravagant beliefs. The criterion is not the delirious idea taken on its own—what idea isn't delirious when taken on its own?—but the force of conviction that accompanies these ideas and hallucinations. No evidence, refutation, or demonstration can succeed in making the slightest dent in this conviction. Understood in this manner, delirium is defined as the creation of a world, but of a private, "subjective," solipsistic world to which nothing in the "real" world corresponds, other than the elements that "send signals" to the delirium. The delirious person is lodged in the heart of a private world, the sovereign occupant at its center.

Given this conception, however, the psychologist Louis A. Sass finds the following paradox to be astonishing: how is it that delirious subjects accept the reality of certain aspects of the external world, even though those aspects enter into contradiction with their delirium? "It is remarkable to what extent even the most disturbed schizophrenics may retain, even at the height of their psychotic periods, a quite accurate sense of what would generally be considered to be their objective or actual surroundings. Rather than mistaking the imaginary for the real, they often seem to live in two parallel but separate worlds: consensual reality and the realm of their hallucinations and delusions."[13] How do they succeed in making these two worlds coexist? The explanation is linked to another characteristic feature of delirium: the delirious subject takes the "objective," real, or common world to be *false*. We often insist on the fact that delirium moves in an unreal and extravagant world, cut off from all external reality; but, in doing so, we overlook the other side of the coin, namely, that when he enters into contact with the external world, even when he does so with the best will in the world, the delirious person believes himself to be confronted with a false, artificial, or illusory world. And here is how the paradox is resolved: the delirious person agrees to interact with the "real" world, but only because he does not believe in its reality. He doesn't submit to the reality of this world, he merely plays along.

Instead of viewing this as a paradox, should we not view this as a struggle, as a perpetuation of the already ancient struggle between the madman and the psychiatrist? The psychiatrist constantly repeats to the delirious person: *you are not in the real world*, your deliria are completely illusory. And the delirious person then responds to the psychiatrist: *you are not in the true world*, your reality is completely false. The former poses the problem in terms of reality, the latter in terms of truth.[14] The psychiatrist's argument consists in saying: there is nothing in your world that could be considered real. The madman's argument consists in saying: there is nothing in your world that couldn't be considered false. The one enforces the authority of the reality principle with his constraints; the other promotes the powers of the false with his deliria.

In certain respects, this is close to the form of struggle Michel Foucault describes in his lectures on *Psychiatric Power*. What the psychiatrist wants above all else is to impose a form of reality on the madman, using all the means he has at his disposal in the asylum, and to such an extent that "asylum discipline is both the form and the force of reality."[15] But the madman never stops returning to the question of truth through the way in which he simulates his own madness, "the way in which a true symptom is a certain way of lying and the way in which the false symptom is a way of being truly ill,"[16] but also through the way in which he rejects the "reality" attributed to the real world. One will against another: the delirious person's unshakeable conviction versus the psychiatrist's resolute certitude.

Dick wasn't mad, of course, but he felt himself to be sufficiently threatened by madness that he tried to have himself committed several times. In addition to periods of depression, he experienced violent psychotic episodes, accompanied by periods of delirium, to which the feverish composition of *The Exegesis* attests. Starting in the 1970s, Dick begins to be confronted with delirious and hallucinatory episodes of a religious kind. He goes through a succession of experiences that greatly resemble the experiences he will put his characters through: his world's reality dissipates, allowing another world to appear . . . Instead of being in California in 1974, he was "absolutely convinced that [he] was living in Rome, sometime after Christ appeared but before Christianity became legal. Back in the furtive Fish Sign days. Secret baptism and that stuff" (*Exegesis*, 33). There is no longer anything real about California; it has become a stage set, maybe even a hologram of the Roman Empire. Maybe our reality is only ever the product of a delirium, subjected as we are to deceptive appearances that conceal the true reality from us, as the Gnostics believed? Maybe we have false memories that will vanish when the resurrection of ancient times, the age of the first Christians, takes place? Are the United States of today no more than a resumption or perpetuation of the Roman Empire of yesteryear? Maybe Nixon's downfall is even a manifestation of the Holy Spirit?[17] A strange eschatology that makes the immemorial past return in the present on the basis of an anamnesis that grows more and more profound, more and more delirious—as was sometimes proposed in the philosophy of the Greeks. It isn't so easy to free oneself from the idea of the resurrection.

Dick is convinced of being locked in a struggle with transcendent beings—extraterrestrials or gods—that have the power to falsify the real, to distort appearances, and to act directly on our brains. It is Descartes's evil genius become SF character, the man of good sense against the master of illusions. We aren't surprised to learn, then, that the main character of the novel *Do Androids Dream of Electric Sheep?* is named Rick Deckard and that he lives in a world populated with machine-animals.

Maybe Dick had to confront religion because it was one of the first means of creating other worlds, of populating them with extraterrestrial creatures (angels, seraphim, demons), and of inventing hitherto

unknown modes of temporality and corporeal metamorphoses (immac-
ulate conception, transubstantiation). Had he wanted to republish the
Old and New Testaments, there was an SF editor who already had new
titles lined up for them: the Old Testament would be called *The Master
of Chaos* and the New Testament, *The Thing with Three Souls*.[18] The
whole question is knowing which type of fiction ultimately wins out in
Dick's work. Is science fiction placed at the service of his religious deliria, or does he succeed in incorporating the latter into science fiction?

The situation is as follows: on the one hand, a succession of delirious episodes that keep him from having a psychotic break but that also
disrupt the "field of reality"; on the other hand, reality is shot through
with all sorts of deliria—economic, political, bureaucratic, and so on—
and "deformed" by them. Dick's stories are like a succession of scenes
depicting the battle he wages against his own madness. This is particularly apparent after the series of religious experiences he undergoes between February and March 1974, when, in *Radio Free Albemuth*
and *VALIS*, he depicts himself through two distinct characters: one who
has just experienced psychotic episodes in the form of religious deliria,
and another, an SF author, who is concerned about the mental health
of the first. Here, we reencounter the confrontation between the madman and the psychiatrist, though we don't always know which character takes on which of these roles. And this same struggle—between delirious possibilities and the prevailing reality—is found everywhere in
Dick's work.

The struggle is as much a war of the worlds as it is a war of the
psyches. There is no psyche whose consistency would not be disturbed
by the intrusion of another psyche. There is no world whose reality

would not be altered by the interferences of another world. Because, for Dick, the plurality of worlds doesn't mean parallel worlds "arranged like so many suits hanging in some enormous closet";[19] they never stop interfering with and impinging on one another, each world contesting the reality of all the others. The war of the worlds is at the same time a fight against madness. If several worlds exist, the question of knowing which of them is real necessarily arises. Once again, the question "what is reality?" is not an abstract inquiry but instead bears witness to the presence of an underlying madness. The madness pierces through the war of the worlds; it makes his characters crack, it distorts objects, makes machines go haywire, and destroys worlds.

Does that mean that Dick *takes the side of madness*, that he fights for the powers of delirium against all the forms of prevailing reality? That would be the function of his "delirious possibilities": to contest the legitimacy of that reality, to denounce its falsity, arbitrariness, and artifice. Hence the many false worlds in Dick's novels. Or maybe he *takes the side of the doctor* and tries to show the extent to which the prevailing reality itself is enclosed within multiple deliria—bureaucratic, economic, political—which all claim to be the one reality, excluding any alternative (*VALIS*)? We clearly aren't dealing with an asylum doctor anymore, but it is nevertheless always a question of mental health—if only, as in *Clans of the Alphane Moon*, to prevent the Earth from becoming a madhouse.

1

Let's take the deliria of Don Quixote. Foucault has described the way in which Quixote's deliria "transform reality into a sign," how the visible beings populating the real world are metamorphosed by the legible signs of the chivalric novel and submitted to an imaginary order.[1] When this transformation fails, Don Quixote can always blame the sorcerers, he can denounce their crafty spells in order to protect the truthfulness of his delirium and to justify it to Sancho. In this way, if the great armies advancing across the plain are, to Sancho, mere flocks of sheep, it is because the sorcerers have deceived him. When appearances go against it, the delirium seals the gaps in order to preserve the cohesion of its world. We therefore understand the role that Sancho plays. With the help of the narrator, he is the one who guarantees the order and coherence of the visible world. He is the man of common sense, solidly anchored in the real world. He only loses his sense of reality when Don Quixote makes his delirious speeches. Then, he is ready to believe anything—and, first of all, that he will become the rich governor of an island. The distribution of roles is well-defined: Don Quixote is the man of words; Sancho, the man of things.

The situation grows more complicated in the second part of the novel, because the characters they encounter have read the story of their earlier adventures. And, as a result, they are able to manipulate reality: they can reaffirm the knight's deliria and satisfy the ambitions of the squire. Reality isn't simply given anymore, it is staged. The world becomes a stage filled with representations. Little by little, representations invade the entire space of the novel: the tricks of the mise-en-scène, the deceptive appearances, and the trompe-l'œil manipulations make up the new theatricality of the world of Representation, *theatrum mundi*. Novels within novels, plays within plays, the alluring interplay of truth and falsity—the powers of artifice have definitively taken the place of the powers of marvel and legend, those old powers dating back to the days when gods and supernatural beings still intervened in the course of the world. Whereas Sancho had previously been capable of pushing back against his master's deliria, he doesn't stand a chance against the deceptions and pretenses of this new world. From now on, only the narrator can guarantee the distinction between reality and illusion; he alone fully controls the distinction (as the reader fully enjoys it). He can play with the trompe-l'œil, make use of the comic and the ironic, make fun of human vanities and passions, and lead his characters astray into labyrinths of appearance and subterfuge. The narrator is no longer the initiate who communicates with natural and supernatural powers but has become the master of Representation and its theaters.

In both parts of the novel, the power of delirium remains within the limits of the world of representation and is distributed throughout its mirror effects and nested scenes. When will the world of representation come crashing down, in turn? This occurs when the narrator discovers phenomena that neither the laws of this world nor the play of false appearances can account for; when he discovers "objectively" inexplicable phenomena. For instance, in worlds where the dead return to life, where phantoms prowl and automata come to life, where the strange, the monstrous, and the abnormal are granted legitimacy, as in the gothic novel or the fantastic tale. It isn't only the characters that are mad, but the world itself that has grown delirious and is "objectively" distorted by inexplicable phenomena, as if at the outer limits of this world an order reigned in which the laws of nature no longer held sway.

And how could the narrator himself possibly avoid being dragged down by such a collapse? It isn't just the world that is "objectively" distorted, but now the narrator too is afflicted with mental confusion and begins to grow delirious, as in "The Horla" or *The Turn of the Screw*. The boundaries separating worlds have become so uncertain, it becomes impossible to know "objectively" whether or not the narrator is delirious. Are there really phantoms in this world or is the narrator just suffering from hallucinations? How can we know for sure if there's no one left to guarantee the "objectivity" of the tale? The narrator leaves the stage of representation to descend into the depths of nature, where he is confronted by new laws, both physical and mental. On one side as on the other, subjectively as well as objectively, there is no longer any certainty.

Both of these aspects of the collapse of the world of representation are to be found in Dick's work. *On the one hand*, making full use of the possibilities SF offers for creating unusual worlds, Dick presents us with worlds that are "objectively" delirious: worlds in which you discover, one morning, that there are extraterrestrial worms hanging from the trees, where you learn that your best friend of many years is actually a warlord from a distant planet, where you wake up in a parallel world in which you don't exist, and so on. However, *on the other hand*, seeing as many of his stories unfold from the points of view of paranoids, psychotics, androids, drug addicts, and extraterrestrials, the distinction between the "objective" world and the "subjective" world can no longer be maintained.[2] There always comes a moment in which we no longer know if the supernatural events of the story refer back to the laws of a new world or to the madness of its characters.

A passage to the limit often occurs, such that a subjective vision transforms into an "objective" reality. For instance, in *The Simulacra*, a schizophrenic pianist, frightened by the idea of absorbing everything he comes into contact with, really makes a vase disappear into his chest. "He scrutinized the desk intently, his mouth working. And, on the desk, a vase of pale roses lifted, moved through the air toward Kongrosian. The vase, as they watched, passed into Kongrosian's chest and disappeared" (*Simulacra*, 194). On the other hand, sometimes it turns out that the "objective" world is ultimately only the projection of one or several psyches. In *A Maze of Death*, we learn that the strange planet explored by a group of colonists is, in reality, a "polycephalic [. . .] joint projection" of the whole group, which never actually left the ship. In other words, the subjective/objective distinction loses its entire raison d'être.

This stems from the fact that his novels adopt a succession of particular viewpoints in order to get "into the characters' heads." The story follows a first character, then a second, and a third, then returns to the first, et cetera. As Norman Spinrad says, his stories are "mosaics of . . . the realities of the viewpoint characters"; there is no preexisting reality, "only the interfacing of a multiplexity of subjective realities."[3] Multiplying the viewpoints does not mean varying the perspectives on a single world but rather multiplying the worlds relative to each perspective. The fictional universe of Dick is a "pluriverse," to use William James's term, a universe composed of a plurality of worlds.[4] If needed, there are even drugs that can "pluralize" worlds.[5]

This isn't to say that the goal of Dick's narrative approach is to show that each character has her own singular vision of the world or that she possesses a world of her own. There is no relativism in Dick. His method really only ever has one aim: it is always a question of *staging a war of the worlds conceived as a war between psyches*. Psyches battle one another in an attempt to impose—or to preserve—the "reality" of their worlds. As Spinrad has already said, we can't even be sure that there is a common world in which they interact, rather than interworlds in which each world would itself be an overlapping of worlds—hence the necessarily multifocal nature of his stories. When a character realizes that she is no longer in "her" world because something abnormal has happened to her, this is the sign that another psyche has burst into her world and warped its organization. Under such conditions, how can a world endure with any permanence? The question that Dick makes the leitmotif of his oeuvre ("what is reality?") stands on a battlefield where psyches fight one another with predominantly "mental" weapons: telepathy, drugs, cerebral manipulation, paranormal powers, the implantation of false memories, manipulations effected through politics, the media, religion, or psychiatry, an so on. All combat is mental in Dick. A few shots are fired with futuristic weapons, it's true, but that's nothing compared to the battles waged by the psyches.

Eye in the Sky illustrates this with great comic force: the world passes through successive transformations according to the moral values, political convictions, and religious beliefs of each of the characters.[6] What guarantees that the confrontation will be a predominantly mental one is the fact that all of the protagonists have actually been in a coma since the beginning of the novel. During an organized visit to a laboratory, they were victims of a particle accelerator explosion. The radiation that engulfed them produced an unexpected effect: the whole group of characters is held captive successively within each individual's mental universe, with the person to whom that mental universe belongs imposing his or her reality on all the others. They pass through the world in which a dogmatic communist lives and through the world of a religious fanatic, where a simple prayer restarts a broken-down car, where a blasphemy immediately triggers an attack of appendicitis (which can only be cured with the help of holy water), and where all of the televisions turn themselves on spontaneously whenever a sermon is on. "As far as I'm concerned, this is an absolutely crackpot universe. [. . .] How can you live with that? You never know what's going to happen—there's no order, no logic. [. . .] We're helpless; we have to depend on whim. It keeps us from being people—we're like animals waiting to be fed. Rewarded or punished" (*Eye in the Sky*, 93, 76).

The situation isn't any better when the characters find themselves in the world of a paranoid woman or that of a puritanical aesthete who decides, in the name of sublimation, to remove all sexuality from her world, deeming it to be vile and degrading. Her world benefits further from the elimination of flies, car horns, meat, Russia, atonal music, cats, and nasty little girls. "In cleaning up the ills of the world, Edith Pritchet eradicated, not merely objects, but whole classes of objects" (129). The other characters then decide to present the realities of the world to her in a form so repulsive that she eliminates them all, one after another, until in the end "her" world disappears entirely.

The conditions that constitute each of these worlds are the beliefs, values, and convictions of each character. From one to the next, reality is transformed: Black people become lazy and illiterate according to the worst racist cliches, women become as "sexless as bees" or turn into devouring monsters, a building's cellar becomes a digestive system, and so on. There is something terrifying about mental worlds, about their way of eliminating entire swaths of communal reality, of transforming them and disfiguring them to the point of caricature. And to be sure, each of the views of the world that Dick presents is closely tied to the context of the United States in the 1950s: a religious fanatic, a puritanical aesthete, a paranoid, and a dogmatic radical—everything the central character has had to suffer in the real world prior to the explosion.[7]

On the other hand, this all means that if a communal reality exists, it is composed of all these terrifying individual visions that can be encountered at any moment in the social realm, like so many worlds within the world. It isn't just the universes of thought and discourse that make the social realm the site where ideas confront one another and a variety of diplomatic transactions take place. Experience is much more violent: we move through a familiar world, communal up to a certain point, a world where we possess an effective reality until the moment when we are projected into a new world that deprives us of all reality, where we are perceived as no more than a caricature, an accessory, a vague and insignificant or possibly harmful presence, or where we aren't perceived at all, where we are invisible. A world where the conditions have changed to such an extent that we no longer have any rights, like in *Flow My Tears, the Policeman Said*, where the main character passes over into a world where he doesn't exist, where he has never existed. Yet it isn't just a nightmare; it is reality itself, a certain part or segment of the world with its specific conditions of existence. The closed world of religious madness, of paranoid hatred, of moral puritanism, and of so many other things besides. We are in "their" world. And we understand why, at the end of *Eye in the Sky*, the main character decides to change his life: it is to change the world. The communal world in which he lived up to that point was always really the site where the four terrifying worlds he just lived through converged: *consensus gentium* or the United States with McCarthyism in full swing.

We have definitively left the grand stage of the *theatrum mundi*. The world is no longer a spectacle given through representation, in which each person plays her role like an actor. It has become an insane asylum, *asylum mundi*: the monologues of actors have been replaced by the deliria of psyches. The controlled play of deceptions and illusions has been replaced by the torments of an uncertain and unstable reality. Individuals have all become deterritorialized, out of sync, and maladapted in relation to the world. We don't need to scour the galaxies to find extraterrestrials. Humans are—literally—extraterrestrials. "The more I learn of other people's thoughts the more universally true it seems that each person has another world in him and that no one really belongs to the world as it is. In other words, we are all aliens. None of us belong to this world; it does not belong to us. The answer is to fulfill one's other world through this one."[8]

Already true of each of the worlds in *Eye in the Sky*, this is even more the case for *Clans of the Alphane Moon*. Alphane is a moon on which various populations live under the distant control of Earth. They aren't aware that their moon "had originally been a hospital area, a psychiatric care-center for Terran immigrants to the Alphane system who had cracked under the abnormal, excessive pressures of inter-system colonization" (28). And, seeing as they weren't even aware that they had been committed, they have overthrown the hospital that they took to be a concentration camp. Very quickly, they succeed in forming a viable society, governed by a caste system—proof, to them, of their sanity. In it, we find the Pares (a clan of rigid paranoids), the Manses (a clan of maniacs, inventors, and warriors), the Skitzes (a clan of visionary and mystical schizophrenics), the Heebs (hebephrenics, ecstatic manual laborers, who live with the Skitzes), the Polys (a clan of polymorphic schizophrenics), the Obcoms (a clan of obsessive-compulsives, who make outstanding functionaries), and the Deps (a clan of depressives, detested by all the other clans).

Because the CIA, back on Earth, fears the ingenuity of paranoids in the political and military realms, the authorities have decided to take back control of this moon. "Frankly, we feel there's nothing more potentially explosive than a society in which psychotics dominate, define the values, control the means of communication. Almost anything you want to name can come out of it—a new, fanatical religious cult, a paranoiac nationalistic state-concept, barbaric destructiveness of a manic sort—these possibilities alone justify our investigation of Alpha III M2" (39–40). For their part, the clans, under the leadership of the paranoids, fear an assault by the earthlings. "They're going to turn us back into hospital patients again" (166).

We quickly realize what Dick is leading to. Clearly, this moon is only a double, an image of the Earth. "How would it differ from our own society on Terra?" asks one of the characters (96). The Terrans are at least as paranoid as their enemies and also live on a hospital-base, populated with schizophrenics and depressives; they, too, are governed by paranoids and managed by obsessive-compulsives. *Asylum mundi.* As in *Eye in the Sky*, reality on Earth is just the interweaving of various mental pathologies and their deliria. If all worlds in Dick are unhinged, it's because they reveal the pathologies of the psyches that have taken possession of them.

2

CAUSALITY

If reality breaks down into a plurality of divergent worlds that interfere with one another constantly, we know that all of the classic categories that organized that "reality" will also necessarily be shattered. How could there be a universal system of causality if phenomena obeying the laws of another world suddenly appeared in this one? How could people be assured of their identities if their psyches were under the influence of other psyches? And even space and time, wouldn't they also need to undergo similar distortions? "Year after year, book after book and story, I shed illusion after illusion: self, time, space, causality, world . . ." (*Exegesis*, 392). If Dick's stories show us the collapsing of worlds, it is because the categories that organize the realities of those worlds lose their status as principles.

The various perspectives of *Eye in the Sky* were already presented as a critique of reality understood as an ensemble of social norms, to which each private world's perceptions, beliefs, and conducts would be subject: reality as *consensus gentium*. How can there be a common world if it is "privatized" by all those who impose their own conditions of existence on it and make it "their" world: political and economic powers, industrial complexes, military and religious authorities? The same thing occurs when reality is understood on the basis of its historicity, beginning with an account of what has *really* taken place. History can be rewritten, falsified. It is even possible to create false archives, like in *The Penultimate Truth*, where the people in power create several versions of the Second World War.

SF is often able to shed the weight of historical reality by making its stories begin after the history of humanity on Earth has already come to an end, as with Asimov's famous psychohistory, the *Foundation* series. That is why so many of SF's catastrophes point in the direction of a possible *posthistory*. But it must also be recognized that there is no SF without *prehistory* or protohistory, as can be seen in the pioneering works of Rosny aîné, which alternate between SF novels and prehistoric novels. Imagining a future beyond history is the same thing as imagining a past before history, and many SF authors make use of these techniques to revive an archaic depth anterior or posterior to history. Dick's oeuvre doesn't stray from this rule, since in it we encounter primitive Martian tribes (the Bleekmen of *Martian Time-Slip*) and Neanderthals (in *The Simulacra*). There is prehistory, posthistory, and even *alterhistory*, such as when Dick imagines that Nazi Germany and Japan won the Second World War in *The Man in the High Castle*.

In each of these cases, it is a question of undoing the determinism of historical reality and of a causal network in which no place is left open for the possible. To be sure, many authors retain a causal network within the worlds they invent, even if those worlds have no relation to our own.[1] This is not the case with Dick. To break with present and past reality, according to Dick, you can't avoid calling the principle of causality, which subtends that reality, into question. "In my worldview (head) there is no appreciation or recognition of causality as normally understood—and I recall that dilemma when I was 19 and found I simply could literally not *see* causality—while all other people do" (*Exegesis*, 241).

If the probabilism of game theory has inspired him since his beginnings—as in *Solar Lottery*, in which political power is randomly granted to a citizen by means of an atomic wheel of fortune—it is because of the range of possibilities it offers that allow him to escape from causal determinism and make it so that every single moment presents the possibility of transforming the world. "Nothing seemed stable or fixed; the universe was a sliding flux. Nobody knew what came next. Nobody could count on anything. Statistical prediction became popular . . . the very concept of cause and effect died out. People lost faith in the belief that they could control their environment; all that remained was probably sequence: good odds in a universe of random chance" (*Solar Lottery*, 17).

But it isn't enough just to loosen the causal framework and substitute the probable for the necessary. The farther he goes in his writing, the more his worlds cease to follow the laws of any physical world, obeying instead the principles—the variable principles—that govern psyches. In this sense, Dick's oeuvre is profoundly idealist. Given a series of inexplicable events, the question is not, what is causing it? but rather, *who* is behind all this? Dickian idealism is another word for paranoia. In the most extreme cases, understanding the laws that govern one of Dick's worlds doesn't mean establishing the constant relations between the phenomena that make up that world, but plumbing the depths of the psyche that controls that world's appearances. All things considered, on an interstellar mission, a psychoanalyst will be much more necessary than a physicist.

And it would be even better if the two combined their strengths and proposed a conception at the meeting point of their respective domains, making the laws of matter join together with the laws of the mind. That may be what attracted Dick to the notion of "synchronicity"—created by the physicist Pauli, then taken up by the psychoanalyst Jung—which he discovered in the early 1960s in Jung's preface to the English edition of the *I Ching*.[2] Synchronicity is the central motor in the framework of *The Man in the High Castle*, which Dick actually wrote with the assistance of the *I Ching*. The *I Ching* rests on the idea that all the events that make up the state of the world at a given moment are related to one another and form a unique configuration, the meaning of which will be revealed to whoever consults the book. "Synchronicity" indicates precisely that momentary configuration that forms the totality of events, both physical and mental. There is no chance, there are only "meaningful" coincidences, which the *I Ching* allows us to decipher if we know how to interpret its oracles. It is no longer a question of inserting yourself into the framework of a universal causal regime but of understanding the place you occupy within the ongoing transformation of the world and the part you should play in that transformation.

In *The Man in the High Castle*, Dick turns to the *I Ching* to substitute methodically synchronicity for causality. As we know, the novel describes an alternate world in which Germany and Japan have won the Second World War and divided the United States between themselves.

The East Coast finds itself governed by Nazi Germany and the West Coast by Japan. Under the influence of Eastern culture, it has become common to consult the *I Ching* and to organize your perception of the world in accordance with its synchronicities. But what does a relation of this kind look like? In what way does it differ from a causal relation? A relation of synchronicity can be observed, for instance, when two characters exert an influence on one another, even though no causal link exists between them. Such is the case when a profoundly troubled Japanese dignitary—troubled because he just shot two Nazi officers with a Colt 44 replica—refuses to sign the deportation form of a Jewish man he doesn't even know, but whom the reader knows to be precisely the artisan who crafted the weapon in question. The two men didn't know one another, they will never meet, but their actions become "meaningful"—they have saved one another's' lives without knowing it—due to their participation in this singular configuration of the world.[3]

According to the *I Ching*, this is more than a coincidence or what Breton called "objective chance." As it turns out, in consulting the *I Ching* that day, the two characters had received the same hexagram. It is therefore the *I Ching* that brought them together and not merely a set of circumstances. The *I Ching* is what distributes the configurations of events, the synchronic states of the world. In other words, the *I Ching* *acts as a psyche.* "We live by a five-thousand-year-old book. We ask it questions as if it were alive. It *is* alive. As is the Christian Bible; many books are actually alive. Not in metaphoric fashion. Spirit animates it. Do you see?"[4] *Deus ex liber*. It really is the "Book of Transformations," the machine that distributes events and reveals their synchronicities.

It is thanks to this book that causally independent parts of the world come to interact with one another and that people understand the role they play in the vast configuration of the whole.

But we need to go further: synchronicity doesn't only bring about relations between distinct parts of a single world, it also creates relations *between entirely different worlds*. Thus, just as Dick writes the history of an alternate world in *The Man in the High Castle*, there is an SF novel—*The Grasshopper Lies Heavy*—circulating covertly within his novel, whose author imagines that it's the Allies that have won the war. If *The Man in the High Castle* depicts an alternate world to that of the reader, our world is an alternate world to that of the novel's characters. Each world is a reverse image of the other, as in a mirror. But these two worlds are separated from one another as the virtual image in a mirror is separated from the real world that it reflects. Here, again, it is the *I Ching* that makes the two worlds communicate synchronically.

This can be seen in the experience that the Japanese dignitary has while transfixed in the contemplation of a piece of jewelry (which was also made by the Jewish artisan). For a brief moment, he is projected into the world where the Allies won the second world war. The Japanese dignitary's interior monologue: "Now one appreciates Saint Paul's incisive word choice . . . seen through glass darkly" (*The Man in the High Castle*, 206). The two worlds enter into communication by virtue of an expanded synchronicity that straddles them both. Thus, it becomes clear that each world feels the effects of the alternate world that it might have been and whose potentialities it continues to carry in its fringes. Nazism isn't a dead possibility, extinguished by historical reality, but continues to flank the present of the United States of the

1950s. What survives of Nazism in a reality that claims to have finished it off?

The central question of *The Man in the High Castle* isn't just, what would have become of the world if the Nazis had won the war? but, in what ways have they won even in a world in which they were defeated? We might say that each world borrows from the other and contaminates it according to the principle of the interconnection of all events, as illustrated by the photograph in *Life* magazine, depicting a family of ordinary Nazis in front of their television set (because, in this world, it was the Nazis who invented television) in the manner of a typical American family. Is it the Nazis who, without knowing it, borrow the kitsch aesthetic of American magazines, or is it the American magazines that borrow from Nazi propaganda and its idealization of the Aryan family? Or is there a murky middle zone between the two worlds, which bears witness to their synchronicity, "seen through glass darkly"?

The principle of causality cannot answer these questions; it cannot explain how something with only a potential existence can nevertheless act on a given state of things, apart from all causality. What Dick is looking for in the practice of the *I Ching* is a system that would allow divergent or alternate worlds to communicate, instead of asserting the sole existence of a single world, whose phenomena would be submitted to a constant and uniform causal order. In other words, he is seeking a system of explanation that no longer rests upon the causal action of *actual* existences, as is the case with universal mechanism, but upon the influence of *virtual or potential* realities, as is the case with psyches.[5] That is why, in Dick's eyes, the *I Ching* is more than just a book; it is at once a divinity, a living book, a psyche, a mega-computer, and a text-machine. Whoever consults it enters data into it (through successive, semi-aleatory draws), to which the book responds with its oracles.[6]

It is sometimes said that idealism presents the world as a book whose signs must be deciphered if we are to understand the grammar of God. As with Bishop Berkeley, the idealist *reads* the world through the ideas she forms of it, which are like expressions of the divine language. But Dick is writing in an epoch where screens have been substituted for books to such an extent that the idealist hardly reads anymore; we should imagine her instead in front of screens, whether televisions or computers. She no longer deciphers a language, she processes information. God no longer speaks the world to himself through the intermediary of ideas and thing-signs, as in Berkeley; he transmits information into brain-screens, which means that, from now on, reality can be manipulated and projected in the form of deceptive holograms. This is one of the (multiple) hypotheses of *The Exegesis*: "So our little psyche-world systems are perpetually bombarded with incoming information which we process and, at the right time to the right other stations we transmit in the rightly modified form—but all this takes place *through* us as if we were transistors, diodes, wires condensers and resistors, all none the wiser" (*Exegesis*, 387).

From this point of view, theories of information have supplanted the old idealism, but they play the same role as the *I Ching*: they substitute, for the cause-and-effect relation, an emitter—receiver relation, which resembles a relation between psyches. Nature becomes analogous to a psyche—or a god—whose messages and codes must be decoded, as biology has done with DNA. God is no longer the grand master of causality; he has ceased to be an artisan, a clockmaker, or a grammarian, to become a programmer. Some might conclude from this that all problems have therefore become problems of communication, and that all we would need to do to resolve them would be to promote new forms of dialogue, inaugurate special parliaments, or found diplomatic authorities. But this won't suffice for Dick, given the incessant war waged between psyches. And if, in *The Exegesis* as in certain novels, there is a war between several divinities, the stakes of their battle will be information, as it is in Wiener.[7] The true information of the Torah, of Christ, of Dionysis, or of Brahma against false information, against the falsifications of false gods or empires (Roman or American). They no longer address the mind, as in Berkeley, they go directly to the brain, like drugs. In Dick's novels, dealers are as powerful as gods because they provide parallel worlds, just as gods are suppliers of realities.

3

THE THINKING THING

In a universe where worlds overlap one another and where "improbable" events strip the principle of causality of its status, how can people be assured of their identity? Wouldn't the principle of identity (I = I) be threatened in turn? Wouldn't people be profoundly affected by the intrusion of other worlds into their own? If the principles of reality and causality crumble, doesn't it follow that the principle of identity would fall with them? As one concept after another *loses its status as a principle*, people no longer know what is happening to them: they no longer know whether the world they live in is real or an illusion, and they find that their identity (who am I?) and their nature (what am I?) have been called into question.

In his *Meditations*, Descartes reasons from the activity of the "I think" to the substantiality of the self as a thinking thing. In Dick, nothing guarantees that the "I" in question couldn't be under the influence of a drug, a paranormal power, or drives issuing from the depths of the unconscious. Nothing can assure me that "I" is really me. Sometimes it's even as if "I" became a sort of intruder, "as if another person or mind were thinking. But different from the way you would think. Even foreign words that you don't know" (*A Scanner Darkly*, 955). What can ultimately assure me that my thoughts aren't coming from some other entity, something that has taken control of my brain?

Descartes discovered the self independently of any relation to a world. He had to suspend the existence of the world for the self to reveal itself in its proper substantiality. But the problem is posed completely differently in Dick's work, almost in the exact opposite terms. If the world were to disappear, that would mean that the self too would lose all substantiality, that it too would dissolve—which is to say, there is a close correlation between the self and the world, for Dick. "A person was his world; without it he did not exist."[1] But beyond this, and unlike what takes place in Descartes, the existence of the world isn't just provisionally suspended; the world really does disappear and the reality that emerges in its place is completely different. "He could see the people, the room also. But he could not identify this place, these people, and he wondered if the breach with that which had been familiar was so complete as to include himself; had his own physical identity, his customary self, been eradicated too, and some new gathering of matter set in its place?" (*Lies, Inc.*, 84).

The deformation or disappearance of the world is a sign of a profound mental disorder, often interpreted in terms of Jungian psychoanalysis—which was much more influential on Dick than its Freudian counterpart. Primordial images rise up from the depths of the collective unconscious that lines the psyche, repressed ancestral archetypes that shape the world, even giving it a hallucinatory form.[2] This collective memory conditions all individual histories despite being repressed within each one. In Dick, deliria and hallucinations always come from far beyond an individual's history. "He has buried it all, and yet it is still there, worrying him like a dog worrying a rag."[3]

In Dick's eyes, the advantage of Jung's theories is that they show the unconscious to have an immediately collective and social, even cosmic dimension, such that mental disturbances are straightaway given a sociopolitical complexion, when they aren't found to stem from even more archaic depths. It isn't individual trauma but contemporary society that produces neurotics, perverts, depressives, schizophrenics, paranoids—paranoids, above all—and everyone feels themselves to be menaced by this foundation of collective drives that lies hidden in the depths of the psyche. "Schizophrenia was a major illness which touched sooner or later almost every family. It meant, simply, a person who could not live out the drives implanted in him by his society. The reality which the schizophrenic fell away from—or never incorporated in the first place—was the reality of interpersonal living, of life in a given culture with given values."[4] Whence the recurring—and often comic— presence of psychoanalysts and psychiatrists in Dick: from the epileptic Japanese psychoanalyst who charges a thousand dollars per half-hour, to another who doesn't realize that his patients are androids; from the psychoanalyst who suggests that his patients leave to live on Mars to solve their problems, to the robot psychoanalyst provided by the authorities, whose function "was to equate people [. . .] with the world as it was."[5] They all fit in perfectly in Dick's delirious universe.[6]

The problem isn't mental but *cerebral*, and takes into account the fissure that traverses the brain and separates its hemispheres. On the one hand, the left hemisphere corresponds to the various "digital" or numeric relations, such as arithmetic and linguistic competence; on the other hand, the right hemisphere corresponds to "analogical" relations, those of paralinguistic or kinesic systems.[7] The one works on discrete unities using logico-analytic algorithms, while the other grasps continuous wholes, *gestalts*, through intuition or "sympathy." All of Dick's characters live on this fault line and face the constant risk of watching it expand to the point of dissociation, leaving them incapable thereafter of integrating the hemispheres in a superior mediating activity.

The most remarkable case is that of Fred, the narcotics agent in *A Scanner Darkly*, who is working undercover as Bob Arctor, a minor dealer, in the hopes of working his way up to the major traffickers, who have introduced a drug with devastating effects into the market.[8] An occasional user himself, Fred is not unaware that this drug produces "a split between the right hemisphere and the left hemisphere of the brain [. . .] and a loss of proper gestalting" (954). His superiors, who are unaware of his double identity—because all narcotics agents wear suits that "scramble" their identities—inform him that they have decided to place Bob Arctor under surveillance. As a result, Fred's mission consists in spying on himself. "Up the street at the house I am Bob Arctor, the heavy doper suspect being scanned without his knowledge, and then every couple of days I find a pretext to slip down the street and into the apartment where I am Fred replaying miles and miles of tape to see what I did, and this whole business [. . .] depresses me."[9] The character progressively succumbs more and more to the effects of the drug until ultimately he splits and, in the end, no longer even realizes that he is investigating himself. "I'm slushed; my brain is slushed."[10] The splitting leads to a complete psychic disintegration, such that, by the end of the novel, he isn't even a person anymore, just a fixed gaze with no life.

Dick often returns to the separation of the hemispheres as if the bicameral structure of the brain were the source of all dissociation and all mental splits. Isn't that what happened to him personally in the 1970s, just after writing *A Scanner Darkly*, when the reality of his world dissipated and he was plunged into the world of imperial Rome at the time of the first Christians? When he caught a glimpse of a gaping rift in the history of the world and saw that his psyche had split? He was no longer Philip Dick, SF author, American citizen residing in California, but a Christian in the year 70. "The concept that I'm a time-traveler from 70 A.D. completely explains Thomas [the Apostle]. The PKD personality is a memory-less mask, and Thomas is the authentic personality of the time-traveler, and hence Thomas is really myself—the *actual* me who was sent here: like a cuckoo's egg. I am not PKD; I am Thomas—there was no theolepsy; only anamnesis. No wonder I could read and write Latin under LSD" (*Exegesis*, 299). Individual history steps aside and allows the ancestral memories of the collective unconscious to re-emerge. As delirious as they are, the innumerable hypotheses feverishly recorded year after year in *The Exegesis* allowed him, as he said, to reconstruct himself, to reassemble himself through his own dispersion. Without a doubt, the function of delirium is to bring the edges of this rift back together, to mend the tear that destroys the psyche. Delirium is always "the attempt at a cure, the reconstruction."[11]

The novels written during this period are often presented as being autobiographical, because they contain descriptions of experiences

Dick himself underwent, including even unaltered extracts from the *Exegesis*. But isn't the opposite the case? He doesn't inject his lived experience into his fictions; instead, his lived experience flings *him* into his fictions. Dick has become one of the characters from his novels. The novelist no longer projects himself into his novels *in his imagination* ("Madame Bovary is me") but finds himself *really* becoming one of his characters ("I'm a protagonist from one of PKD's books").[12]

And that is really what happens in two novels of the *VALIS* trilogy.[13] "Philip K. Dick" actually becomes a character in a novel; in fact, he becomes two. Which is to say, he cannot become a character. In *Radio Free Albemuth*, he is Nicholas Brady, who undergoes the same delirious religious experiences that are reported in the *Exegesis*, but he is also Philip K. Dick, an SF author, who is rather skeptical of his friend's stories. Not only does he give no credence to the idea that an extraterrestrial intelligence exists, but he is concerned about Nicholas's mental health. "That was more than I could manage; the whole thing seemed unnatural and terrifying to me, something to be fought with all one had at one's disposal. The supplanting of a human personality by—whatever it was" (*Radio Free Albemuth*, 56). He even comes to think that his friend is suffering from a dissociation of his cerebral hemispheres, like the agent in *A Scanner Darkly*.[14]

Something similar takes place in *VALIS*, again with two distinct characters: Horselover Fat, which is a rather rough-hewn homonym, and Philip Dick, who drives the first person narrative.[15] The former is half-crazy: he is writing an exegesis because he believes "that the information fired at him and progressively crammed into his head in successive waves had a holy origin" (*VALIS*, 188). As for Dick, all he can see in this jumble of hypotheses are the signs of a mental disorder, from which he hopes to save his friend Fat. When Fat explains to Dick that the source of all religions stems from the Dogon cosmogony, because it's there that we find three-eyed invaders with the elongated skull of Akhenaten, Dick thinks that his friend has lost all contact with reality. Here, again, we find the dyad of the madman and the doctor, a strange *cogito* in which the roles sometimes get reversed.

This dyad is all the more unstable because the distinction between the two characters tends to be blurred. Even the narrator himself doesn't always succeed at keeping them straight.[16] The split is interrupted when, in the presence of a child with divine powers, Dick realizes that Fat is only a projection of himself.[17] Yet Fat reappears later on, as if a definitive reintegration were possible. "Fat's madness had returned" (*VALIS*, 375). Dick can only be himself on condition that the split exists, being himself and Fat at the same time. "I am Horselover Fat, and I am writing this in the third person to gain much-needed objectivity" (*VALIS*, 177). A principle of nonidentity is therefore established (self ≠ self), just as synchronicity had previously established an acausal principle. What had at first been a founding certitude (self = self) becomes an insoluble problem (self ≠ self?) or an irreparable scission (self = other) before transforming into a plural identity (self = him). Schizophrenia looms over all of Dick's characters, when it hasn't already overtaken them completely. There is always an other in the self, whether in the form of an extraterrestrial or paranormal possession, or in the form of unconscious drives that threaten the integrity of my psyche.[18]

It is true that Descartes does not pose the question of personal identity. That problem belongs instead to Locke, who founds personal identity upon the continuity of memory. I know that I really am myself as long as there exists a continuity of memories, a continuity that is guaranteed by a ceaselessly renewed act through which the contents of consciousness assimilate to one another in such a way that I am made to say: that is really me.[19] But, in Dick, the self doesn't have any more continuity than it has substantiality. In the first place, this is because many of his characters suffer from periods of amnesia. The gaps in their memories introduce profound ruptures in the narrative framework. Dick's stories are not always continuous; they are strewn with holes, as if perforated. Characters leave their apartments like always, only to find themselves suddenly on a spaceship, in a hospital room, or on a distant planet, without knowing what happened in the interval. Were they asleep? Were they drugged? Were they hallucinating? Did they go mad?

The problem is exacerbated as soon as it becomes possible to implant false memories into people's brains. This is what happens in "We Can Remember It for You Wholesale," in which the protagonist can no longer distinguish between real and false memories. "—'Did I go to Mars?' he asked her. 'You would know.'—'No, of course you didn't go to Mars; you would know that, I would think. Aren't you always bleating about going?'—He said, 'By God, I think I went.' After a pause he added, 'And simultaneously I think I didn't go'" (S5, 204). The means of distinguishing between real and interpolated memories is lacking to such a degree that, even if the continuity hasn't been broken, it becomes uncertain. And like on the individual level, the collective level of historical reality has also become the object of a variety of manipulations, interpolations, and occultations. For Dick, history is characterized in the first place by its falsifiability, as in *The Penultimate Truth*, in which the people in power make use of various falsified archives, including several versions of the Second World War that they can use as the need arises.[20]

Not all of Dick's characters go as far down the path of psychic disintegration as the agent in *A Scanner Darkly*, of course, but many live in such a state of dissociation that they no longer feel any emotion at all. Dominated by their left hemispheres, these characters become purely rational beings, devoid of empathy and guided by a purely abstract logic. In such cases, then, we aren't dealing with the problem of their identity anymore but the problem of their *nature*, which is to say, of their humanity, as if they've been cut off from a part of themselves and transformed into inhuman creatures. The problem is no longer: who am I? but: *what* am I? Descartes referred the "I think" back to a "thinking thing," sure. But what is the nature of this thing? Man or machine? Dick often said that, along with the question, "what is reality?," another question also haunted him: "what is it to be human?" His fear isn't that machines will replace humans but that humans will transform themselves into machines. The danger isn't the mechanization of bodies, nor the automation of thoughts, but *the dehumanization of psyches*.

This can be seen in "Imposter," which tells the story of a man who is arrested outside his home on the suspicion of being a robot created by extraterrestrials to destroy Earth. There is supposedly a bomb inside of him that will explode as soon as he utters the code phrase. The man protests: he really is himself. But how can he prove it? "That was the whole trouble. There wasn't any way I could demonstrate that I was myself," (S2, 374). The man escapes the security officers, but, as he flees, he discovers his own bloody corpse. That's when he speaks the detonation phrase: "But if that's Olham, then I must be—." So, the "thinking thing" was a machine, after all.[21]

Being a "thinking thing" doesn't at all guarantee being human if a robot gets the job done just as well. What's more, a human whose left hemisphere has become dominant—a human whose ability to communicate verbally, to calculate, and to manipulate discrete and coded unities has developed, at the expense of his feeling for the intuitive, "sympathetic" relations based in the right hemisphere—becomes inhuman, a sort of android. He is enclosed in a world of abstract relations. He is the modern schizoid, "the overtrained cerebral person," deprived of emotions. "He was a young man, with a competent no-nonsense expression, a thoroughly detached schizoid person indeed" (*The Simulacra*, 65).[22]

Like the principle of causality, the principle of identity (self = self) cannot be maintained, because a constitutive rift in the brain constantly threatens to grow wider and to spread everywhere, to crack worlds open, to split individuals in two, and to make them lose their humanity or hurl them into psychosis. All of the deliria in Dick's works are born of this rift through a tireless struggle for recovery, a ceaselessly renewed attempt at reconstructing a "self," that sends his characters, who are gnawed at by madness and drugs, wheeling through worlds that collapse the moment they are created, in the hope that this grand dispersion will allow him to gather everything back together again.

4

ON THE FANTASTIC

Dick often returns to the distinction between waking and sleeping starting from the Heraclitean distinction between the common world (*koïnos kosmos*) and the private world (*idios kosmos*), which, for him, functions as an equivalent of the distinction between the normal and the pathological.[1] When we think that we're in the delirious world of some character, sometimes it turns out to be a common world, shared by others; and when we find ourselves in the real world, sometimes it turns out that it is actually the product of a delirium—and that's not even to mention the stories in which the question remains wholly undecidable. Perhaps the schizophrenic, the addict, and the paranoid are living in private worlds, but they just might also have access to a reality in which ordinary people would be reduced to a state of waking slumber, willfully partaking in the illusion of belonging to a common world.

What Dick rejects above all is this strict distinction between worlds. SF thinks with worlds, it invents worlds, but what is most essential, for Dick, are the interferences that take place between worlds. That's why, in many respects, he is closer to fantasy than he is to SF. To be sure, there are aliens, spaceships, and distant galaxies, but those aren't what's most important in his work. If we had to establish a distinction between them, we could say that SF envisions *a* world (or several), while fantasy always brings about a collision between *two* worlds (or more). SF can be rational in the way it conceives of worlds, but fantasy is always confronted with the irrational, because a collision between worlds will always unsettle the distinction between the real and the unreal. And it is precisely in this state of indecision the fantastic is to be found.

From this point of view, Todorov is right not to limit the fantastic to a fixed literary genre, connecting it instead to a singular kind of experience that would be independent of all genres: namely, to those moments in which the character no longer knows whether the supernatural event she is witnessing is a sensory illusion or perhaps a product of her imagination, which would mean that the laws of her world still hold, or if instead the event actually belongs to the framework of reality, which would then mean that it obeys the laws of some unknown world.[2] This is often what happens in Dick, even if everything is explained in the end. There are countless situations in which we no longer know which world the event that is unfolding belongs to. It is an experience that is close to the "uncanny," which Freud understood rightly as a confrontation between two worlds: a disquieting world finds its way into the familiar world and threatens to destroy its order.[3] When a world suddenly changes, it is a moment of fright. The imagination fails: all you can say is that you have perceived something $= x$ that comes from another world—something inexpressible, but something *real*.[4] Dick's greatest successes are of this kind. How dreadful, the world has been breached! "I'm sorry, Mr. Bolero, but there's a creature under your desk."[5]

From this perspective, it isn't clear that the Heraclitean distinction between dream and reality is still applicable. Philosophy has long raised the question of the dream, but without really believing what it was asking. When it asks if reality isn't just a succession of linked dreams, one has the strong suspicion that this is a rhetorical question and that no one seriously doubts our ability to distinguish dreams from reality. From this point of view, phenomenologists are right to say that the "grain" of a dream will never have the same consistency of waking perception.[6] The distinction between the two worlds wasn't really threatened. But was that even the goal? If philosophy has long pretended to dream, it wasn't to call reality into doubt, but, first and foremost, to provide a basis for the authority of judgment and establish its superiority over every other form of thought. Though Socrates has his demon, Plato his visions, and Descartes his dream, dreams and visions are always intruders in the mind of the thinker. Judging, that is the only legitimate activity of thought, the only possible definition of thought such that it protects us from dreams and deliria.[7]

Now, the first activity of judgment consists precisely in *distinguishing between worlds*, determining which world is the real one, and then finally distributing beings within the worlds. The sleeper who awakens, freed from the extravagances of her dream, knows that she is back in the real world first of all because she has regained her faculty of judgment: so it was all just a dream. She can once again distinguish between what is real and what isn't, between the true and the false, the certain and the probable, and so on. She can once again trust that her perceptions, beliefs, and statements bear upon the "real" world. Conversely, it will be said that the dreamer is not of this world. Sartre describes her as having withdrawn into a "closed consciousness," deprived of being-in-the-world. The dream's images don't form worlds but "atmospheres of a world."[8] Here, judgment takes full advantage of its jurisdiction over the two worlds. The reality of the world isn't a matter of givenness but of jurisdiction. How else do we make sense of the fact that reality, far from being given, must be raised to the level of a principle: the famous "reality principle."[9]

It will be objected that the reality of the world is a self-evident fact that precedes all judgment, that it pertains to a primordial belief or a "perceptive faith" that is prior to all determinate judgment. Judgment would therefore find its basis upon the "universal ground of belief in a world which all praxis presupposes, not only the praxis of life but also the theoretical praxis of cognition. The being of the world in totality is that which is not first the result of an activity of judgment but which forms the presupposition of all judgment."[10] But how do we fail to see that this "universal ground of belief" requires us to have already distinguished between worlds, between a real, self-evident, indubitable world and those other worlds that are considered chimeric, fictional, unreal . . . ?

Doesn't this "primordial belief" actually belong on the side of the dreamer? Phenomenology doesn't grant enough importance to the experience of the dreamer, not even to the phenomenology of dreams, which can only grasp them from the vantage point of the waking state. Isn't what characterizes the dreamer really a profound credulity, a credulity even more profound than "perceptive faith," because it isn't rooted in the ground of a preexisting world? If the dreamer lacks being-in-the-world, isn't that precisely what allows her to believe in whatever happens, without being surprised by anything? At this point, there isn't anything unreal, false, or impossible anymore, because the waking, judging self has disappeared: it is asleep.

So, the self of the dreamer comes alive, it spreads itself out and scatters into "a mosaic of blasts." Its unity, which is created through connections rather than integration, is decentered and multiplied.[11] "The subject of the dream, the first person of the dream, is the dream itself, the whole dream. In the dream, everything says 'I,' even the things and the animals, even the empty space, even objects distant and strange which populate the phantasmagoria."[12] Maybe it isn't even necessary to hold onto an "I" anymore, because now it is everywhere, anonymous and multifocal. This isn't to say that the dream immerses us in the unreal or gives us access to the surreal; rather, *everything in the dream is real*, precisely because judgment no longer plays a part in it: the dreamer no longer needs to decide what is real or not, true or false, feasible or impossible. Everything is real, everything is believable, even the most delirious episodes.

Conversely, judgment only sees distinctions, separations, and exclusions. It is constantly engaged in the activity of dividing up worlds or domains. It only asks one question: where to draw the dividing line? Isn't that what characterizes the worlds of *Eye in the Sky*? Each person constructs an authoritarian and delirious world according to the most unforgiving judgments and the most arbitrary norms and values. Each decrees his or her own causal laws, changing the existing world with the removal or addition of entire swaths of reality. They alter its cosmology, reestablish geocentrism, abolish sexuality, eliminate monetary systems, introduce angels or monsters. . . . Judgment decides who takes part in a world and who is excluded from it on the basis of values, norms, and convictions.

By right, the individual who judges never sleeps. She is an insomniac by nature. To judge is to keep watch, to be ever vigilant, a guardian of boundaries. Boundaries always need guardians, including night watchmen. And, as Bergson says, if keeping watch is tiring, it is because you spend your entire day judging, exercising your good sense. "This choice which you are continually accomplishing, this adaptation ceaselessly renewed, is the essential condition of what you call common sense. But such adaptation and choice keeps you in a state of uninterrupted tension. You take no account of it at the time, any more than you feel the weight of the atmosphere. But it fatigues you in the long run. Common sense is very fatiguing."[13] When evening falls, everyone returns to sleep except for the insomniac, who stays awake or wakes up in the middle of the night with the endless vigilance of a judge. Anyone who is able to sleep has been worn out by the activity of judging. What rests is sleep itself, but the dream doesn't belong to sleep. It is a third state, between waking and sleeping. It is the vigilant waking state's other, in which you don't just take a break from judgment, you are freed from it.[14]

We encounter this third state—which does not belong exclusively to the dream—in many of Dick's stories. It is brought about by diverse means: drugs, psychological disturbances, hypnosis, mental manipulation.[15] It is typical of the experience of the fantastic (or of the uncanny). Behind all the various decor that unites his work with the SF genre—behind the desolate planets and distant galaxies, behind the arsenal of spaceships and technological discoveries, and the extraterrestrial creatures—Dick is constantly looking to get back to this experience of the fantastic. It is a zone in which worlds overlap, fall apart, and bifurcate, and in which characters enter into communication with an "insensible substance" somewhat like the state of receptivity into which the cinema sometimes sends us. We might think of Artaud's description when he conceived of cinema as a privileged means of accessing the fantastic. "A whole insensible substance is taking shape, yearning for light. The cinema is bringing us nearer to this substance. [. . .] Cinema will come closer and closer to the fantastic, that fantastic which appears ever more to be the real in its entirety, or else it does not exist."[16]

Why does Artaud's declaration make us think more of Lynch's films than those of the great oneiric filmmakers such as Kurosawa, Buñuel, or Cocteau? Precisely because, in the works of the latter, the dream is understood as a world apart that doesn't interfere with the real world or only does through the play of symbolic or phantasmatic correspondences. Their works put forth a poetics or a phantasmatics that is all the richer because it encloses the dream in the unreal or the surreal. In this way, the dream loses the uncanny power of the fantastic that otherwise allows it to insinuate itself into the real and interfere with its contours. There is an alternative at the heart of the dream: either it is an imaginary world, destined to go beyond the world, to enchant it, symbolize it, or surrealize it; or else, on the contrary, it possesses an insistent, uncanny reality that reveals the rifts in worlds both mental and physical. In the first case, we know that we are in an unreal (phantasmatic) world; in the second, we ask ourselves if we haven't tumbled into another world, but one just as real as the first (fantastic). If the one is linked to the powers of the imagination, the other is linked to the dangers of madness.

In this regard, the weakness of many SF films lies in the fact that they struggle in their attempts to make another world exist or to make the boundaries of this world felt. They can certainly film wars between worlds, the destruction of worlds, and virtual worlds destined to supplant the real one, but this doesn't change the fact that everything in them is perceived on the basis of a preexisting world: the world in which the camera is found and whose reality is affirmed by it. One of the great strengths of Lynch's films is that *the camera itself brings about the shift* toward the limits of the world, toward the indistinct zones that communicate with other worlds; it travels down dark hallways, moves among the trees of a forest, or follows a facade, without knowing if what it is going to encounter will still be of this world or if it will belong to another. In other words, Lynch's camera no longer guarantees the reality of a world; it circulates between worlds, returning occasionally to the sites where they interfere with one another, to their common limits, as if his aim were to film the limit that merges with the zone of the fantastic itself.[17]

Only in this zone are the categories of judgment suspended. In it, causality, identity, and reality lose their status as principles. And that is precisely what happens in Dick's works. As with Lynch, the fantastic is turned less toward dreams and oneirism than toward madness and its dangers. Dick's problem isn't the dream but delirium and its underlying psychosis. A dream is never as terrifying as a delirium, never as dangerous. The dreamer won't be mistaken for a psychotic; still less will the psychotic be mistaken for a dreamer, as was the case in nineteenth-century psychiatry. On the one hand, reality is temporarily suspended (but always ultimately regained); on the other, it collapses (and is never definitively restored).[18]

In Dick's work, we are in a fictional universe where judgment can no longer exercise its authority or can only do so in a completely arbitrary manner. Worlds deteriorate, become disorganized, and communicate with one another in irrational ways. Along with judgment, "perceptive faith," belief in the world underlying all judgment, also disappears. With the collapse of this transcendental confidence, reality as a whole crumbles, as in the case of the psychotics described by Binswanger, which had such an influence on Dick. *As if there were no longer any foundation*, the reader can no longer know whether she is dealing with a strictly mental universe, whether the reality presented to her is "subjective" or "objective."

Take, for instance, the driver in the story "Retreat Syndrome," who is pulled over for speeding and declares that he is sick. "Everything seemed unreal to me. I thought if I drove fast enough I could reach some place where it's—solid" (S5, 88). The police officer is rather skeptical. In a show of good faith, the driver sinks his arm into the dashboard. "You see? It's all insubstantial around me, like shadows. Both of you; I can banish you by just removing my attention from you" (S5, 89). Still trying to convince the officer, he tells him that he believes he has killed his wife; but his psychiatrist, on the phone, tells him that she is still alive, on Earth, in Los Angeles. Yet, he remembers having killed her. Maybe it's a false memory? A hallucination? According to him, he isn't on Earth but is being held prisoner on Ganymede, and his wife is really dead. His psychiatrist assures him that it isn't the case. "Perhaps that was the modus operandi by which the delusional system was maintained; he was being given Frohedadrine in small regular doses, perhaps in his food. But wasn't that a paranoid—in other words psychotic—concept?" (S5, 102). The psychiatrist ultimately concedes that the man is actually on Ganymede, but his wife really is alive. So, he'll have to kill her a second time. He gets in his car and starts off for Los Angeles, when a police officer . . .

One of the conditions set by Leibniz for the existence of a world was that all of the events produced therein must be compatible with one another. Of two things, *one*: if Caesar crossed the Rubicon, then it isn't possible that he didn't cross it. If a Caesar exists who didn't cross the Rubicon, he doesn't belong to this world but to another possible world. The problem Dick's characters face is that they are confronted with situations in which events that cannot be reconciled within a single world occur together. "Is Runciter dead or isn't he? Are we dead or aren't we? First you say one thing, then you say another. Can't you be consistent?" (*Ubik*, 746). The man no longer knows if he is living in a world in which he has killed his wife or in a world in which he hasn't killed her yet. Have I killed my wife or not? Did I go to Mars or not? Am I living or dead? Each time, the response is the same: *both*. We know that Dick doesn't distinguish strictly between SF and fantasy, because most of his stories culminate in properly fantastic episodes where the vacillation between worlds outweighs all else.[19]

Simondon and Deleuze have rightly shown that the Leibnizian law of identity only works at the level of preformed, already constituted individuals. It is true that, at that level, it isn't possible both to have killed your wife and not to have killed her, to be both guilty and innocent, both living and dead. "That's it, he said to himself. I've died. And yet I'm still alive" (*The Simulacra*, 120). Everything is different when we descend to the level of a preindividual reality, where the "reality" of the world is not yet constituted or breaks apart under the effects of psychological disturbances, drugs, or superior powers. At the preindividual level, we are no longer dealing with a preformed world but with an *informal* world in which individualities come undone and incompatible realities overlap and communicate fantastically with one another. This preindividual world is a world of fluctuation and uncertainty, which is to say, a world that contains several worlds, *each as real as all the others*.

Maybe this is the "secret love of chaos" that Dick speaks of? As one character puts it: "Either this is an exhibit on R level of the History Agency, or I'm a middle-class businessman with an escape fantasy. Right now I can't decide which." But he immediately corrects himself: "I've been putting up a false question. Trying to decide which world is real. [. . .] They're both real, of course."[20] This is the meaning of the concepts "inclusive disjunction" in Deleuze and "metastability" in Simondon, where the *fluctuatio animi* reveals that we are "caught between several worlds."[21] For his part, Dick certainly encountered this idea in Jung, since, in the depths of the Jungian collective unconscious, "opposite qualities are not yet separated" and the "bipolarization into paired opposites" has not yet been established.[22] If his worlds fall to pieces so quickly, it is because there is no solid ground, no "universal ground of belief," as Husserl would have it. They are constructed upon a zone that makes them drift and crumble. His characters straddle different worlds; they only live in them for a moment, being in the one only on condition of being already caught in another.

5

ENTROPY AND REGRESSION

No matter, their little gimmick with the dust is charming.

SAMUEL BECKETT, "FIRST LOVE"

SF has often been defined in terms of its way of imagining technological and scientific "progress." But if that were the case, a book like *Ubik*, which revolves almost entirely around regression, the dissipation of energy, and destruction, could hardly be called an SF novel. From this point of view, *Ubik* is the SF antinovel par excellence. Every kind of "progress" is annulled in it, thanks to a strange, even paradoxical temporality. *On the one hand*, the characters are subjected to a violent acceleration of time, which makes them age prematurely. They find themselves overcome by an extreme lassitude; soon, they are dragging themselves along like elderly people, and then they die and crumble into dust, all in less than twenty-four hours. *On the other hand*, a temporal inversion affects ordinary objects, specifically those that are the products of technological "progress."[1] "His stove had reverted. Back to an ancient Buck natural-gas model with clogged burners and encrusted oven door which did not close entirely. He gazed at the old, much-used stove dully—then discovered that the other kitchen appliances had undergone similar metamorphoses" (*Ubik*, 724).

All technical objects begin inexplicably to regress. Spaceships turn back into jet planes and then into "the old biplanes with their huge wooden props"; ultramodern race cars turn back into automobiles from the earliest days of their history. *Ubik* goes against one of SF's deep underlying tendencies, namely, the tendency to populate its worlds with objects arising from technoscientific "progress." Once again, *Ubik* is the antimodel of the standard SF novel, its antitype: everything in it regresses, and what does progress only progresses toward degradation and death. "Reality has receded; it's lost its underlying support and it's ebbed back to previous forms" (*Ubik*, 744). As we said, there is no longer any ultimate foundation. Accelerated regression and precipitated aging destroy the very substance of the world. Once again, the world comes unhinged and ultimately collapses.

If the zone of the fantastic can be likened to the preindividual field described by Simondon and Deleuze, it is because the latter is the source of incessant geneses and transformations. The information that traverses this field, understood as "a difference that makes a difference" (to use Bateson's phrase), spreads, grows, and develops to the point of constituting worlds, forming mineral, vegetable, and animal individualities. Contrary to this, regression takes place whenever a difference no longer makes any difference at all and joins back up with the undifferentiated, in which everything is leveled, blurred, and unmade. Transformation and metamorphoses have become impossible and time's dimensions all say the same thing: "gubble, gubble," as the child mutters in *Martian Time-Slip*. It is the "tomb world" that Binswanger described in *The Case of Ellen West*, which left such a mark on Dick: when the psyche falls into a dark hole, gnawed at by the same entropy that undoes the organization of the universe.[2]

The abyss into which certain psychotics fall puts them into direct contact with the tendency toward undifferentiation that is at work in the cosmos, a catatonia connected to entropy. It is no longer the psychotic depths of the characters that distorts the reality of the world; now, *the world itself possesses a psychotic depth* to which certain "special" people have access. Behind the apparent order of the real, there is another world, equally real but closer to chaos and undifferentiation, that threatens to disintegrate everything it touches, like a sort of anti-world.[3] Regression isn't just a step backward or a fixation on the past, it is also a vision of a future based on the generalized disintegration of all psychic and cosmic organization. The time after rejoins the time before as a return to the inorganic, as with the death drive in Freud. We are far from the image of science fiction as a vision of technological and scientific "progress."

This is what happens when characters come up against forces that prevent them from communicating with the external world. "It is a splitting apart of the two worlds, inner and outer, so that neither registers on the other. Both still exist, but each goes its own way." (*Martian Time-Slip*, 149) More than an interruption, this is the disappearance and absorption of the world within a sort of vortex, as with the experience of little Manfred, the schizophrenic child in *Martian Time-Slip*, who is trapped within a space-time that petrifies him. His perception of time is so accelerated that the world he perceives is constantly eroded by destruction and death, by what he calls "gubbish." Other people appear to him as corpses and the world appears in ruins. When he draws his visions, he represents the future as a desolate landscape of ruins and slums. This elderly child is one of the characters who live in the "tomb world," which is connected directly to cosmic entropy. "It was no escape; it was a narrowing, a contracting of life into, at last, a moldering, dank tomb, a place where nothing came or went; a place of total death" (*Martian Time-Slip*, 128).

Manfred emanates such an immense psychic energy that his presence acts as a veritable attractor; he draws people to himself and awakens psychotic tendencies in them that lead them into states similar to his own, as if they were caught in the accretion disk of a black hole. "It's starting to seep over us and replace our own way of viewing things, and the kind of events we're accustomed to see come about now somehow *don't* come about," (*Martian Time-Slip*, 142–43). And that is exactly what happens to the characters in *Ubik*: the reality of their world is deformed by the psyche of a young man, who absorbs their vital energy in the manner of a black hole.

Little Manfred only sees a world of ruins because nothing can resist entropy: it will eventually disintegrate everything. The ultimate regression is the end of the future, a future emptied of all possibilities. Everything has already happened, *the future is finished*. For the elderly child, there is no longer any difference between the dimensions of time. Whichever way you turn, there is nothing but a dismal, undifferentiated present in which nothing at all will ever happen. The difference no longer makes any difference. "Now I can see what psychosis is: the utter alienation of perception from the objects of the outside world, especially the objects which matter: the warmhearted people there. And what takes their place? A dreadful preoccupation with—the endless ebb and flow of one's own self. [. . .] It is the stopping of time. The end of experience, of anything new. Once the person becomes psychotic, nothing ever happens to him again" (*Martian Time-Slip*, 149).

As Stanisław Lem emphasizes, the regressions in Dick are not the result of an inadequate imagination in which a distant future would see humanity regress to a feudal or prehistoric state.[4] There are, of course, the occasional pockets of prehistory in Dick, as with the autochthonous Martians in *Martian Time-Slip* or the recording crew in *The Simulacra* that encounters a Neanderthal in a long-abandoned, radioactive region. "—'I would think a long time [. . .] before I'd plunk my life down in this area. But if you could do it—you'd have accepted one of the most difficult aspects of life.'—'And what's that?' [. . .]—'The supremacy of the past.'"[5] These parts of the world that are deprived of all future do not belong to a parallel time; they are contemporary with the zones of "progress" observed elsewhere and are the sign that regression threatens reality at all of its levels.

"Kipple," "gubble," or "gubbish": the terms the characters use change but always refer to the same underlying process, pointing toward the identification entropy = psychosis. It is in the greatest depths of mental and physical worlds that its power reveals itself. It can take the form of a passive nihilism, in which the regression is deliberate and desired, as with the striving to return to an inorganic state that characterizes the death drive in Freud. This is what happens to the young woman in *The Ganymede Takeover*, who undergoes a sensory deprivation treatment in the hopes of being freed from all of her neuroses and rejoining the peace of the undifferentiated. "I'm the entire universe and just a single tiny eye, watching," (*The Ganymede Takeover*, 110). I have become matter again, undifferentiated flux, without conflict, oh nirvana!

For certain paranoids, this nihilism can take on a much harsher, active form that transforms into a terrifying political vision. Not only do they see the future, like the "precogs," whose minds are capable of seeing or predicting the future, but they push precognition all the way to the end of time, to the end of everything. More than a vision, though, *this is a desire*, a desire for the end of the world as the supreme victory.[6] Death is the certitude that comes from the future, neither feared nor awaited but desired, ardently desired as the final truth offering absolute vindication, the figure of supreme authority. "Death itself has such authority" (*Martian Time-Slip*, 60). These characters therefore embody the archetype of the "authoritarian personality," for which the sacrifice of oneself (and everything else) becomes the sole strategy for assuring the preservation of a fatal ideal. Health is identified with annihilation.[7] Sure, they will also die, but what does that matter when it proves that they were right and that they were part of the victorious camp? Isn't truth more important than life? Hence that abominable cry—"long live death!"—since death is their ally in that final victory that is really only a victory for death itself. Is there anything more important than being right? Desiring nothing for the future other than the spectacle of destruction and death is one of the main forms of nihilism in Dick's work, with precognition taking on the death-driven look of a fascist nightmare. "Precognition did not lead to freedom but rather to a macabre fatalism."[8]

This gives rise to terrifying visions, as in "Null-O," which tells the story of a gifted boy, "a perfect paranoid, without any empathic ability whatever" (S3, 165). He doesn't think that he has lost touch with reality but that, on the contrary, he is in direct contact with the real, because he has been freed of all the ethico-cultural inhibitions that hinder human thought.[9] Hence, his theory: the world isn't composed of objects, there isn't any individual reality—the "null-O"—but only a "gestalt, a unified substance, without division into living and non-living, being and non-being. A vast vortex of energy, not discrete particles! Underlying the purely artificial appearance of material objects lies the world of reality: a vast undifferentiated realm of pure energy" (S3, 167). His greatest desire is to rejoin the null-O by setting off more and more powerful bombs until the total destruction of the world has been achieved, until "all distinction between land and sea had been lost" and "the surface of the Earth was a single expanse of dull gray and white" (S3, 170). The undifferentiated is the ultimate truth. This dreadful nihilism, which lies at the heart of all regression and pursues certain of Dick's characters, is a desire to have done with all forms of life, to see nothing in the future except the end of all things as the great apotheosis.

There was a danger tied to the world of judgment, namely, that of living only *in a single world*, of ruling out any and all communication between worlds and therefore, for Dick, negating the pluriverse. But this danger is inseparable from another: *anyone who only lives in one world wants the destruction of all worlds, including his own*. Maybe that is the ultimate meaning of the phrase "there is no alternative" (TINA), where it is a question of destroying all worlds for the sake of a single one. Negation becomes destruction, pure and simple. For, if only one single world remains, it too will be condemned to disappear, to devour itself from within, because it lives off the destruction of other worlds alone. The puritanical aesthete from *Eye in the Sky* is perhaps the exemplary case of this: she destroys everything that displeases her in the world, to the point of ultimately destroying her world and herself along with it.

If there is another SF author for whom entropy is as omnipresent, it would have to be J. G. Ballard. But the situation is profoundly different between the two. We encounter the idea again, in Ballard, that the mental and the physical make up one single reality.[10] The interior world and the exterior world have become indiscernible, but in quite a different manner than in Dick. For Ballard, the phantasmatic inner world spreads itself out completely into the external world, into the advertisements, garish lights, and huge megacities, through a generalized pornography and voyeurism. Accordingly, the nihilism in his works no longer needs to be profound, it no longer stems from the archaic ancestral depths; on the contrary, it spreads out before us, around us, and is visible everywhere.

What is the object of an endless struggle in Dick has become, for Ballard, an asset, perhaps even a condition: his worlds are deprived of all "progress"; in them, regression, stagnation, and destruction reign supreme. This can be seen, even in his earliest stories, in the relation between time and matter. This is already true of *The Drought* but also of the splendid *The Crystal World*. In the former, it is the dryness of the Earth, its dust, that thrusts humanity into an unlivable ancestral age. It is another version of "the ubiquity of the dust" that is invoked by the idiot in *Do Androids Dream of Electric Sheep?* (448). In *The Crystal World*, we enter into a region of the world where everything—vegetables, animals, and humans—crystalizes, as if trapped in immense glaciers. But the growth of the crystals takes place less in spatial dimensions than in temporal ones. "It's as if a sequence of displaced but identical images of the same object were being produced by refraction through a prism, but with the element of time replacing the role of light."[11] Time begins to grow in two directions at once, toward the past and toward the future, like mirror images, while encasing the present in the crystal of an eternal death.

SF has often portrayed humans being petrified in matter. That's what happens in *The Crystal World* but also in *The Drought*, where humans can hardly be distinguished from the dust that covers them, coating their faces with dry masks.[12] SF stories often grapple with temporalities that exceed the totality of human time, which requires them to consider both the prehistory and posthistory of human time simultaneously, making the flow of human historical time into a sort of parenthesis or alternative. This aspect has been present since SF's beginnings, as can be seen in the two directions of the pioneering works of Rosny aîné, a novelist of both prehistoric and posthistoric times. This is also the meaning of Ballard's forest: "this illuminated forest in some way reflects an earlier period of our lives, perhaps an archaic memory we are born with of some ancestral paradise where the unity of time and space is the signature of every leaf and flower."[13] If the prehuman time is idealized, the posthuman time is not; on the contrary, its materiality dissipates all ideality.

This is because humanity has lost its cosmic continuity. All around humanity, there is a generalized atomization, a dispersion caused by a great wind that sweeps across a soon-to-be uninhabited Earth, reduced to hostile elements that are as indifferent to humanity as humanity is to everything whatsoever, even including its own destiny—a great gust of nihilism that strips the erotic from everything other than destruction and the void, like in *Crash*. Humanity is a sick fragment of discontinuity that can only be healed by the death that will restore it to the peaceful continuity of the material world. Life and matter are capable of continuity, but humanity no longer is. As Robert Smithson says, "I am convinced that the future is lost somewhere in the dumps of the non-historical past"[14]—closed highway ramps, ambiguous plots of land, wastelands, abandoned buildings, burnt out cars: a deserted world, as if humanity has had enough of life on Earth.

In the future, humanity won't be there anymore; we see that in these deserted zones, where *the end of the world has already begun*. These images are strictly contemporary with the tawdry images of industrial and postindustrial development, those phantoms of prosperity and luxury that temporarily mask them or push them back to the periphery. Luxury—moribund luxury—only has one function: concealing the poverty behind its blinding radiance. Property, riches, and luxury appear to be particularly vain. If entropy is winning, it is because humanity is already dead and affectively defunct: hence the strange taste his characters have for mortal danger. The aspects of entropy we find in Ballard are not, then, the same as those presented in Dick. If, for the latter, entropy sometimes appears in the guise of a demon or an evil deity, it is because humanity is actively fighting it—instead of resigning itself to its desolate triumph, as in Ballard.

THOSE WHO POSSESS WORLDS

—They will never take over and run *my* world.

—You don't have a world. You have an office.

PHILIP K. DICK, *FLOW MY TEARS, THE POLICEMAN SAID*

Take the following Dickian theorem: *every world belongs to a psyche*; and also this variation: every world belongs to several psyches, which together compose a collective, "polycephalic" world, as with the colonists in *A Maze of Death*, who think they are exploring a new planet, when it is actually just a collective mental projection. Or there's the community of addicts in *The Three Stigmata of Palmer Eldritch*, who partake in a communal artificial world around Barbie dolls. This is another way of saying that all worlds are mental. Corollary: *a world belongs to whoever produces or controls that world's appearances*. As long as appearances obey the conditions set by a particular character—her habits, her knowledge of the laws of nature—it can be said that we are dealing with "her" world. She has an idea, even if only a vague one, of what is possible and what isn't, of what is probable and what is improbable, and so on, in this world. All the more so if she alters appearances as she pleases, if she has an effect on them; if, in short, she freely exercises her will upon them. Then, she lives in a world that she knows, transforms, and masters.

An illustration of this can be found in the story "The World She Wanted." A strong-willed, capricious young woman announces to a man, whom she has just met, that he is a part of "her" world. The man is shocked. "You see, Larry, there are *many* worlds. All kinds of worlds. Millions and Millions. As many worlds as there are people. Each person has his own world, Larry, his own private world. A world that exists for him, for his happiness." What's more, she tells him, without asking what he thinks, that they are going to get married soon, because they are in "the best of all possible worlds—for me. [. . .] You have a world someplace else, a world of your own; in this world you're merely a part of my life. You're not completely real. I'm the only one in this world who's *completely* real. All the rest of you are here for me. You're just— just *partly* real" (S2, 175–76). The entire world depends on her desires; she has the power to decide what is real and what isn't. If something doesn't interest her, if it bores her or belongs to a distant past, it doesn't exist or only partly does.[1] Yes, the world is my representation—until the man realizes that he can remove her from "his" own world.

By right, each person controls the appearances of her world and can decide which are real, which are unreal or illusory, et cetera. Like the young woman from the story, many of Dick's characters have fantasies of omnipotence; they dream of living exclusively in their own worlds, where they would decide everything and act with a total, uncontested sovereignty in the manner of gods. The same thing happens when these worlds are created by several minds. This is the case with businesses,

State apparatuses, and religious organizations: they collectively create worlds whose limits are fixed and whose appearances are controlled.

Only, with Dick, the situation quickly grows more complicated. How do you claim to live in a world of your own when your world has come unhinged, when its appearances begin to slip out of your grasp and inexplicable things begin to take place, as, for example, when one is on drugs? For Dick, this is a clear sign that someone is in the process of taking control of your world. You can always say that the effects of a drug are fleeting. But if you become dependent on the drug, this means that the dealer has indirectly taken control of your world. Ketamine, amphetamine, dopamine, anything will do. He will provide you with the appearances and the "reality" that you previously lacked; but then your world belongs to him. This brings us back to our corollary: *every world belongs to whoever produces or controls that world's appearances*—it belongs to whoever decides for you what should be considered real, important, and essential.

It will be objected that drugs don't produce anything real. But how do you know? What makes us so sure that the opposite isn't the case, that we aren't brainwashed at birth and only drugs allow us to see the situation clearly, as in the story "Faith of Our Fathers," in which aliens have invaded Earth and given humans a hallucinogenic water that conceals reality from them? Only a drug allows them to lift the veil and discover the truth.[2] The same is true of madness: what makes us so sure that schizophrenics don't have access to a greater truth? "My writing deals with hallucinated worlds, intoxicating & deluding drugs, & psychosis. But my writing acts as an *antidote*—a detoxifying—not intoxicating—antidote."[3] This confirms that a world belongs to whoever controls its appearances, whether that be a political power (terrestrial or extraterrestrial), an industrial power, a god, a dealer, or beings with paranormal powers.

A passage to the limit takes place in Dick's works, which merges with the limits of SF itself. We can certainly say that the brain in withdrawal belongs to the dealers, that the lungs and arteries of the smoker belong to the tobacco industry, that labor power belongs to the economic powers that buy it. But these examples only concern parts of a world that exists within a vaster preexisting reality. The passage to the limit takes place when one is dispossessed not just of certain parts of the world but of the totality of the world itself. The problem then becomes onto-theological. It is the very reality of the world that stems from another psyche, just as religions conceive of the world as a divine creation. The world becomes a projection, a broadcast scheduled by a superior psyche. Hence the close correlation between gods and dealers in Dick, since dealers share with gods the power of creating a new world from scratch.

This means that, in Dick, appearances aren't given; they are always produced by some psyche or being. There is no being-in-the-world, because we are always already in the world of another. Nothing is ever given, everything is always transmitted, broadcast, projected. Here, Dick's idealism joins up with theories of communication that understand our interactions with the world to be like a relation between psyches or pseudo-psyches communicating messages to one another. The world no longer has its own independent reality. What we call the "external world" is only the common limit or the interface between various systems of communication. The terms of the relation are no longer

thought on the basis of the subject/object duality but of the trans-
mitter/receiver duality, of which the world is only the interface.

In other words, the relation between a human and the world *is a relation between two psyches*, the world itself being a psyche, a pseudo-
psyche, or an ensemble of information produced by a superior psyche.
How could information theory not have suited Dick, who understands
everything to be a war of the psyches? We know that he came to understand the world as a projection, a hologram, or an artifice projected
by a god or an extraterrestrial power. This communication between
psyches favors the alliance between cybernetics and religion that one
finds in Norbert Wiener's *The Human Use of Human Beings*, which Dick
read closely. Again, God is no longer the Author of the great book of
nature, whose signs must now be deciphered by humanity. He has become the Transmitter and the Producer of a gigantic televised broadcast. "To take it—i.e., the world as authentically real would be the same
as taking a TV image and program and its dramatic contents—as real"
(*Exegesis*, 284).

What is the Passion of Christ if not another televised program?
"Christianity is like a given drama on TV; what I've been trying to figure
out for 6-1/2 years is not what this one drama of many is about, but
how the TV set works that brings *this* drama" (*Exegesis*, 619). In several
stories, Christ becomes a televisual character whose calvary is broadcast by means of "empathy boxes" that allow spectators to enter into
a new world; they momentarily merge with the false Christ and participate in his virtual Passion.[4] In *Do Androids Dream of Electric Sheep?*,
this televisual Christ has a rival in a very popular comedic television
host. "He and Wilbur Mercer are in competition. But for what? Our

minds, Isidore decided. They're fighting for control of our psychic selves" (488). In the background, there is always a war of the psyches.

Once again, the situation of the idealist has changed. She no longer sits with a book, she sits in front of screens. What we call "the world" has become the transmission of information, images, sounds, or informative units, however discontinuous (bits) or continuous (gestalts) they may be. Beyond televisions, there are also computers, which only make interactions and communications more intense. The entire world enters into the machines, passes through the screens, and is digitized. "There is a whole huge map room of computer info, input and output from [our world], continual traffic."[5] This is one of the primary operations of the *Exegesis*: to couple information theory with theology.

Berkeley had pushed idealism to the point of immaterialism, but the new informational idealism puts its full faith in dematerialization. It is the great promoter of dematerialized existences. Every form of existence is reduced to packets of information, completely digitized and injected into a great variety of programs. This new doctrine must be called dematerialism. It isn't a negation of materialism but its denial, its perpetual numeric abstraction. This new doctrine's program? A generalized dematerialization and informatization of the world. Matter has lost its thickness and its opacity; it has become transparent because it communicates its data and its messages can be deciphered. And that is ideally true of all matter: brute matter, but also sensible matter, affective matter, cerebral matter. All kinds of matter become transparent and communicative. "It was living hell in the twenty-first century. Information transfer had reached the velocity of light."[6]

That is why there are so many telepaths in Dick: the brain has become transparent, making it possible to read your neighbor's thoughts. Because individuals give off as much information as they receive, it isn't even necessary to have recourse to paranormal powers anymore. Informatization allows for a total transparency: "He slid his key into the slot; it registered, and now the ruling monad, after consulting its memory bank, knew and remembered every source item he had ever utilized, and in what sequence; it comprehended the entire pattern of his formal knowledge. From the archives' standpoint, it now knew him without limit, and so it could declare [. . .] the next point on the graph of his growing, organic, mentation-life. The historic development of him as a knowing entity" (*The Penultimate Truth*, 61).

If each individual is reduced to a packet of information, it becomes possible to know more about him than he knows himself. This is the end of all private life and all anonymity.[7] Even the slightest movement you make is detected by systems of control that hold sway over every aspect of existence. Dick is very aware of this constant control over the lives of individuals and senses its increasing development. "How many other blips are we setting off, or our children will be setting off, in contexts that we know nothing about yet? [. . .] The kids of today, having been born into this all-pervasive society, are fully aware of and take for granted the activity of such devices."[8] Societies have become vast societies of control, and individuals, "living things turned into data sold by the inch" (*The Zap Gun*, 118).

This digitization or dematerialization has a correlate: the increasing artificialization of worlds and their inhabitants. This is the great, analogical principle of the theory of information: matter, lives, thoughts, and machines are understood from the perspective of the information that they receive and transmit. To be sure, intelligent machines are only tools and only have an analogical relation with living and thinking forms. Their "intelligence" is only the implementation of a retroactive process of autoregulation. It goes without saying that such machines only have artificial life and intelligence. And yet, *on the basis of this very artificiality*, there is no longer anything that distinguishes them from living forms or forms of thought as far as the transmission of information is concerned.[9] "The synapse in the living organism corresponds to the switching device in the machine."[10] We don't, of course, confuse the barista with the coffee machine, but confronted with the metaphysical enemy that is entropy, all differences vanish: we are united against the common enemy. Considered in terms of information, life, humanity, and machine all move to the same plane, beyond their differences of nature. The analogy spreads in both directions: machines are *just like* living beings and living beings are *just like* the new machines. The theory of information lets us artificialize all forms of existence. Everything is communication! Everything is artifice! Machine humans and human machines.

Cybernetics and information theory thus present themselves as *a metaphysics of—and for—artificial worlds*. If it really is a question of metaphysics, it is because there is a gigantomachy of Order and Disorder unfolding in the background. But the legitimation of the artificialization of the world is not this metaphysics' sole function; it also has the objective of legitimating the development of new technologies of control within the social field. Considering the aptitude intelligent machines have for calculation, prediction, and control, as well as their trustworthiness in carrying out tasks and programs, it is imperative that they be integrated into the social field as active participants and that new human-machine complexes be created. They are indispensable weapons in humanity's cosmic fight against entropy.

The intrusion of cybernetic machines into our lives thereby receives its metaphysical legitimation: they are on our side in the daily struggle against the disorders of entropy and therefore help us adapt ourselves to the social environment created by "progress."[11] Entropy alone justifies all the new technologies of control. Information is another name for forced adaptation.[12] In other words, the androidization of humanity obeys a necessary metaphysics. "I suspect that the tyrannical machines will be introduced into our lives in a gradual, insidious way . . . through the service entrance, so to speak. They certainly won't have signs reading 'Danger'. More likely, 'At your service' [. . .]. But it won't be long before the bill is sent to the happy owner, because in our society you have to pay to be reduced to slavery. That's what is most insulting."[13] The artificial worlds of capitalism really are like amusement parks, and entry isn't free.

All of Dick's observations point in the same direction. The objective of these new technologies is not to transform the existing world but to replace it with artificial worlds, to make us live in "false" worlds, whose appearances will from then on be controlled. We are going to take possession of your world, we are going to dematerialize it and artificialize it, so as to take control of it; we will be able to alter its appearances and impose our terms of use on you to make you a part of it, and so forth. Advertising, the media, and computers all appropriate the "external" world by making it disappear behind billboards, glowing screens, and cardboard-cut-out towns. But they are just as interested in appropriating the "internal" world of psyches. That is the real objective of these artificial worlds: to control brains, the way drugs do. If you control the transmission of information, then you're in control of what gets called "reality." The world belongs to you.

There are no soft drugs in Dick. There are only hard drugs that attack the brain directly and take control of it, as in Burroughs. That's why drugs become a religion, a religious experience, just as religion had been the opium of the people.[14] The drugs/religion parallel is particularly present in *The Three Stigmata of Palmer Eldritch*, where the two drugs in circulation are sold by two dealers described like rival divinities. The first is a drug of communion: people merge with Barbie-like dolls, allowing them to escape from the harsh life of the Martian colonies. "Many of the colonists find in the drug itself a religious experience that's adequate for them" (340). It is the Host that the characters take in order to pass over into a standardized world, controlled by the dealer. The Barbie-doll world becomes a sort of manger for junkies.

The second drug introduces us into a world that seems much more "real" than the fake dollhouse world, the space-time of which is under the exclusive control of the dealer. His slogan: "God promises eternal life. We can deliver it" (361 and 306). The trade-off is that you aren't able to free yourself from that world; you are permanently at the mercy of the dealer's caprices, a sort of depraved god capable of altering the world at will. There is no longer a distinction between the real world and the altered world, as there was for the first drug; you can never be sure if you have truly returned to the real world. Gods and dealers have in common that they are both purveyors of other realities. If dealers have a divine power, it is because they put new realities on the market that allow them to take control of psyches and hold them captive. Like the faithful, addicts enter into a world that was made for them, but that always belongs to another.

What Dick's multiple worlds show is that the way in which worlds are possessed has changed. In a general manner, governing a world used to consist in establishing or maintaining an order in the sense of a *form of organization*. The world was created once and for all, its matter organized according to defined forms. Following this hylomorphic schema, the form of organization preexists the matter that it organizes by right. Only the world whose populations submit to this preexisting form of organization can be called "real," which means that any phenomena that don't submit can be excluded or downgraded, considered to be illegitimate claims. Governing means, then, imposing the authority of an exclusive form of reality. Conversely, reality gets conflated with this form of organization's ensemble of imperatives. "If psychologists turn up in the school, the factory, in prisons, in the army, and elsewhere, it is because they entered precisely at the point when each of these institutions was obliged to make reality function as power, or again, when they had to assert the power exercised within them as reality."[15]

What happens when it is no longer a question of form but of information, when the world is reduced to being an interface between transmitters and receivers? We no longer maintain the reality of a preexisting world; on the contrary, the world must be continuously produced. We no longer impose a preexisting, organized form, but have substituted for it the flux of information of a perpetually transforming world. Deprived of all foundation, the world becomes unstable and precarious. But this instability, this fluidity is what demands and "justifies" that control be exerted from start to finish, from the transmission all that way to its reception. To this end, those in power no longer impose a form, but demand ceaseless transformations.[16] Reality doesn't preexist anymore; it is produced through the multiplication of artificial worlds, designed to guarantee the control of psyches. *The war of the psyches has become a war for the control of information*. And that is what SF should describe. "The continued elaboration of state tyranny such as we in science fiction circles anticipate in the world of tomorrow—our whole preoccupation with what we call the 'anti-utopian' society—this growth of state invasion into the privacy of the individual, its knowing too much about him, and then, when it knows, or thinks it knows, something it frowns on, its power and capacity to squash the individual— as we thoroughly comprehend, this evil process utilizes technology as its instrument."[17] To be sure, States are no longer the only ones exercising such powers, but the point remains the same: using technology to control lives.

7

ARTIFICIAL WORLDS

I guess we expect difficulties in living,
but there ought to be some sort of limit.
PHILIP K. DICK, *THE SIMULACRA*

Of all the worlds created by Dick, most numerous are the "false" or artificial worlds. Perhaps that's why worlds collapse so easily in his work. The false insinuates itself everywhere: false worlds, false humans, false memories,[1] hallucinations, deliria, android psychoanalysts, and electric sheep. This can be seen as a consequence of Dick's paranoia, but it is also a fact of American society in the 1950s, with the appearance of television, the invasion of advertising images, huge shopping centers, and amusement parks like Disneyland—a whole series of artificial universes that took over the social sphere and contaminated all other worlds. The United States—and California in particular, where Dick lived for most of his life—became, for him, bound up with a "fake" reality, "a fun park for grown-up kids."[2]

"But you see, Mr. Lem, there is no culture here in California, only trash. And we who grew up here and live here and write here have nothing else to include as elements in our work; you can see this in *On the Road*. I mean it. The West Coast has no tradition, no dignity, no ethics—this is where that monster Richard Nixon grew up. How can one create novels based on this reality which do not contain trash, because the alternative is to go into dreadful fantasies of what it *ought* to be like; one must work with the trash, pit it against itself, as you so aptly put it in your article. [. . .] Hence the elements in such books of mine as *Ubik*, If God manifested himself to us here He would do so in the form of a spraycan advertised on TV."[3]

"Pitting the trash against itself" is perhaps one of the best descriptions ever given of Dick's oeuvre. It means, in particular: include advertising techniques within the story itself, construct worlds as artificial as those found in the amusement parks, build reconstructions as fake as those of the casinos in Las Vegas. This is what aligns Dick as an author with pop art. If Ballard can be likened to minimalism and Smithson, Dick is resolutely on the side of pop.[4] It isn't that SF pulps belong to pop culture in the same way as Lichtenstein's comics or Oldenburg's hamburger. But there is a common promotion of the false, of the "trash" or "kitsch," a similar proliferation of objects and images that occupy the same space as signs and billboards, like so many literal reproductions of the current consumer products of American society. This is especially true of *Ubik*, certainly the most "pop" of Dick's novels, with each chapter being preceded by an advertisement and money as fake as the bills made by Warhol or Lichtenstein circulating throughout the book.[5] Reality has become completely artificial, or rather, as pop irony would have it, the artificial has become the new reality, which must now be reproduced as *literally* as possible.[6]

In this sense, pop art is the exact inverse of minimalism. Minimalism fights against the supposed European "illusionism" in favor of a literality that acts as an ultimate truth at the limit of tautology. Hence, Frank Stella's famous formulation: "*What you see is what you see.*" A painting is nothing other than a painted surface, and this flat, literal truth is what must be depicted, stripped of all "illusion." The same literality is found in pop, though it is no longer thought of as the presentation of a bare truth, but as the promotion of a falsity, of a generalized artifice that is being endlessly intensified and amplified. We are no longer dealing with orderly, emptied-out spaces, occupied by pure, isolated forms that confer a voluminosity, or even a new theatricality, upon the emptiness, as in minimalism (unless, of course, these forms open us onto the dangers of entropy and the "tomb world" of Ellen West?).[7] Pop space, on the contrary, is saturated with images; it is a full space, overrun by the trivial images of the social sphere, all the "kitsch" of mass culture. In one of the first exhibitions of Warhol's work, visitors progressed down narrow hallways between piles of Brillo boxes, Kellogg's cartons, and cans of preserved fruit, like in a "fake" supermarket.[8] The repetition that proliferates itself, the multiplication of images and portraits destined to fill up every space, is one of the essential aspects of Warhol's work. And then there are Oldenburg's giant objects and the increased scale of the comics in Lichtenstein. Everything takes place as if the minimalists isolated essences in order to better reveal their truth, while the pop artists made appearances proliferate in order to better reveal their emptiness and artificiality.[9]

A *first* aspect that places Dick's novels in conversation with pop is the intrusive presence of advertising. In his universe, aliens are less invasive than advertisements, like in *The Simulacra*, where living ads the size of flies try to get into a car to deliver their sales pitch to the driver. "The ad agencies, like nature, squandered hordes of them."[10] But the story that best illustrates the intrusive and invasive power of advertising is "Sales Pitch," which tells the story of a man returning home from work on Ganymede, after his daily commute of millions of kilometers, throughout which, each time, he is accosted auditorily, visually, and mentally by advertisements of all sorts. The man has only just arrived home when a multifunctional robot shows up and launches into a series of comical demonstrations, like a traveling salesman who is trying to sell himself. "They always wanted a product that sold itself, didn't they?" (S3, 219). The robot destroys the furniture, digs a tunnel through the floor to show how to escape an attack, punches a hole through a wall to show how to knock out intruders and thieves, and dumps all of the food onto the kitchen floor, only to repair the damage while also modernizing the appliances, painting the walls, and spraying all of the rooms with a gas that kills toxic bacteria. Completely fed up, the man demands that it leave immediately. The robot's response: "I'm not your fasrad to order around. Until you've purchased me at the regular list price [. . .]. You'll feel better after you've turned responsibility over to me" (S3, 220–21). This robot single-handedly incarnates the intrusive force of advertising in Dick, as well as its insistence that it knows, better than the consumer herself, what she truly desires, since everything has already been thought of for her, for her comfort, taste, and pleasure, on the basis of scientifically studied standards—the promise of a new world.

A *second* aspect that puts his work in conversation with pop is the omnipresence of replication and what it reveals of the false or "trashy" nature of a given reality. Anything can be replicated, and it can either take place within a single world or even between two different worlds, as with the photo of an ordinary Nazi family, "watching television in their living room," in the alternate *Life* magazine in *The Man in the High Castle* (68), which is a double of the same image in our world. There are even pop aliens whose sole function is to replicate manufactured objects, like the creatures in *A Maze of Death* that "duplicate things brought to them. Small things, such as a wristwatch, a cup, an electric razor" (70). Or the Martian amoeba in *Now Wait for Last Year* that takes the form of a mink stole through mimetic replication. And then there are the Biltongs in "Pay for the Printer" (S3), which love replicating objects, even though, as they grow old, they end up making useless approximations.

Whether by doubling or division, everything can be reproduced. Even humans can be replicated and recreated—the ultimate pop— hence the characters that Dick fittingly calls "simulacra" and, later, androids. In *We Can Build You*, a factory has even recreated Lincoln and his secretary of war, Stanton, and they are as human as the originals. There are fake humans just as there are synthetic toads and sheep in *Do Androids Dream of Electric Sheep?* And there's Molinari, the dictator in *Now Wait for Last Year*, who uses replicas of himself, which come from parallel worlds, as clones or spare bodies. As in Burroughs, the "trash" has the propagative power of a virus; and like a virus, it brings with it a sickness, the malady of an artificial reality that spreads until it becomes the one and only reality.

Little by little, the proliferation of these images attains such power that they eventually come to constitute veritable worlds. The fact that these artifacts lead to the creation of totally artificial worlds is what most interests the SF author. Again, Dick isn't only a contemporary of pop art, he is also a contemporary of the delirious urbanization of Los Angeles, the cardboard cut-out reconstructions in Las Vegas, and the creation of amusement parks like Disneyland. "Unceasingly we are bombarded with pseudorealities manufactured by very sophisticated people using very sophisticated electronic mechanisms. I do not distrust their motives; I distrust their power. They have a lot of it. And it is an astonishing power: that of creating whole universes, universes of the mind. I ought to know. I do the same thing."[11]

Indeed, the creation of artificial worlds reaches new levels of intensity with Dick. In his early stories, the artificial worlds are usually miniaturized worlds or model cities that suddenly become real, as in "Exhibit Piece" (S3), where the archivist disappears permanently into the model of a twentieth-century city, or "Small Town" (S2), in which a man who builds a model of his town ultimately traps his wife and her lover in it.[12] They can also be false worlds designed for therapeutic purposes, like the world into which the psychiatrist in *The Man Who Japed* sends his patients. "He was not in a fantasy world. [. . .] He was on the Other World, the permanent refuge maintained by the Mental Health Resort."[13]

These worlds can also be nostalgic artifacts. Fredric Jameson has emphasized the importance, in Dick, of collectors who amass objects from contemporary American culture, like movie posters, Zippos, Mickey Mouse watches, and old Colt revolvers, which are coveted not just because they are rare but because they allow them to reconstruct a bygone world. The nostalgic dictator in *Now Wait for Last Year* wants to reproduce the Washington, D.C., of his youth on Mars. Likewise, the main character of *Time Out of Joint* unknowingly lives in an artificial reconstruction of a 1950s village (while the novel takes place in 1998).[14] Everything you desire becomes immediately attainable, like in a regressive dream of childish omnipotence. "The hallmark of the fraudulent is that it becomes what you would like it to be. [. . .] Your world obliges you, and that gives it away for what it is."[15]

Yet, it is doubtful that Dick's aim is to give the present of the 1950s and '60s a new intensity by granting it a "posthumous actuality," as Jameson thinks.[16] Dick is actually after the opposite effect: to reveal the trash and the artifice of the present to which he is contemporary. Otherwise, it would be hard to understand why the collector characters gather the most ordinary objects of the era. If, in the future, the present of the 1950s and '60s, which is now a historical reality or antiquarian fetishization, can be reconstructed—or counterfeited—perfectly, it is because it was already artificial when it was the present, as artificial as a Mickey Mouse watch, as if it were already a parody and an artifact of itself.[17]

The false, the artificial, is not just something that comes in and distorts or deforms the "true" and "authentic" world; *it achieves an autonomy that grants it a new reality*, a reality that competes with all the others and uses its invasive strength to supplant them. It doesn't cut itself off from the real world but substitutes itself for it. Invasion means: we are the new reality that has replaced the old, and from now on you live in this world. You won't see anything but these appearances, which have been designed especially for you. This new world unleashes a permanent propaganda that allows it to capture, shape, and standardize desires and beliefs, and therefore, in short, to make itself desirable. Everything in it is false: appearances, languages, social functions, faces—but what does that matter when they have become the one and only reality? Above all, as with drugs, you have to pay to have the right to take part in this world. Your beliefs and desires will be all the more intense because you will have invested everything you have in them, "because in our society you have to pay to be reduced to slavery. That's what is most insulting."[18]

The moment a world gains autonomy, the appearances it creates no longer need to be related to another reality or to truths other than themselves: in constituting *a single* world, they no longer refer to anything beyond themselves, in a permanent state of self-referentiality. It is an open system, but one that runs on a closed circuit, like a world enclosed beneath a geodesic dome.[19] Information necessarily becomes redundant, because this world no longer resonates with images other than its own, in a perpetual state of self-promotion.[20] We have fully entered the realm of generalized self-promotion. "Life in Anaheim, California, was a commercial for itself, endlessly replayed. Nothing changed; it just spread out farther and farther in the form of neon ooze" (*A Scanner Darkly*, 884). Because this new, artificial world imposes its visual and auditory images directly on psyches, there is no longer any distinct, "inner" world that might escape the invasion. Psyches link clichés and standardized images to one another and, in doing so, become artificial humans. Worlds become artificial and then make everything populating them artificial, "falsifying" their existence.

There are countless decoys and false appearances in Dick, from the long-dead "first lady," whose idealized image has been perpetuated by actresses, to the android serving in the place of an elected political leader, and from falsified historical archives to fake news. Thus, in *The Penultimate Truth*, world leaders convince the Earth's population, which is crammed into underground shelters, that the planet has been ravaged by an interminable war and that the levels of radioactivity in the atmosphere have left it uninhabitable. From their shelters, the people watch the war unfold on giant screens. "This was their window—their sole window—on the above world, and they took rather seriously what was received on its giant surface" (12).[21] But, in reality, the war ended long ago, and the ruling class only maintains the illusion to keep the planet's riches and livable zones for itself: they had committed "the theft of an entire planet from its rightful owners" (49). This was already the strategy used by those in power in *1984*: make the people believe in an ongoing war, so as to legitimize yourself and subjugate the population. In Dick, everything is false, not just the images but the computer-generated speeches that pronounce the officially held truths, the android president who delivers those speeches on television, the fake films that are broadcast to make people believe that the war is still raging—politicians, engineers, technicians, intellectuals, everyone participates in the construction of this artificial world. "The problem is a real one, not a mere intellectual game. Because today we live in a society in which spurious realities are manufactured by the media, by governments, by big corporations, by religious groups, political groups. . . . "[22]

In this case, the reason for creating the "false" world is clear: it is a decoy intended to capture the beliefs and desires of the population and to divert their attention away from the real world. To be sure, you can always say that everyone lives in "their" own world, but Dick never stopped fighting against this simplistic form of subjectivism, because the "reality" of the world is not a theoretical problem but the object of concrete political struggles. How are psyches deceived, *how are they robbed of the world* and of their own relation to it? Which images, discourses, and psychological manipulations will do the trick? And if it is necessary to use drugs to do it, which ones?

Any method is fine, as long as the population is wrested from the Earth and reterritorialized elsewhere, whether in religious tales, artificial worlds, television programs, advertising images, or wherever else it might be. The attraction just needs to be sufficiently strong to turn them away from the real world. Stealing worlds, stealing the Earth: isn't that the very operation by which all colonization functions? The technological means used in Dick's novels to steal worlds, to conceal their "reality" or dispossess their inhabitants of their lands, are like the endless aftershock of the primordial earthquake upon which the imitation universe of the United States has been built: the theft of an entire continent from its inhabitants, with the Mayflower playing the role of the alien invaders' ship. That is what most of Dick's invaders do; they take over a planet and then conceal the theft with the help of screen-worlds. But that is also what humans do with regard to their own planet. Instead of living on it, they have colonized it—which is why, in many of Dick's stories, the Earth has become uninhabitable, forcing them to migrate and colonize other planets.

The colonist isn't just the person who appropriates the land and its inhabitants; she also imposes a new reality on them, like missionaries imposing their god on populations of infidels or heretics—though, in

Dick, they use technological and pharmacological means. This substitution consists either in destroying the old order for the sake of a new reality, deemed "superior" in light of the "progress" it has brought about across all domains, or in maintaining the appearance of the old reality while destroying it in secret (for instance, maintaining an appearance of democracy while working tirelessly to destroy it). In the first case, it is a question of colonizing the natives, in the second, of colonizing the colonizers themselves. These two modes of colonization correspond to the two stages of the colonization of North America: first, with respect to the "Indians," on whom a new world is imposed, and then with regard to the Americans, on whom the fake world of the *American way of life* is imposed.

This is particularly apparent in *Martian Time-Slip*, in which the natives, the Bleeks, live in a different temporality than the one in which the human colonizers live. They belong to the time before the colonizers, before modern humans. They are like the Indians, who continue to haunt the United States and who make it a country that has been "false" from its very beginnings, built as it is upon the perennially repressed primordial lie of primitive accumulation and populated with individuals who are ever more deterritorialized: the trash of the *American way of life*. The strength of the native Martians lies in the fact that they don't live according to the destructive, irreversible time of capitalism. Their temporality is at times too fast, a vibrant kaleidoscope of colliding images, and at times too slow, idle and beyond repair. Only young Manfred, the schizophrenic child, is capable of entering into their unique temporality.

The function of falsified appearances is to enclose individuals within a sheltered world that only ever receives images of itself. The creation of an artificial world produces a profound caesura, a division that gives rise to a horrifying alternative: either the amusement parks of capitalism and the theft of "an entire planet from its legitimate owners" or the camps of marginalized people, pushed to the periphery, invisible or underground. The existence of camps—or of reservations— is the sign that the world does not belong to everyone. The excluded no longer have a world, and yet they really are real. They are the reality that the artificial worlds don't want us to see. That is why they are forced into camps or lawless zones, as in *Lies, Inc.*, where a fascist-style mega-corporation uses a one-way teleportation system to send colonists to a distant planet, which turns out to be an immense work camp.[23]

Are you in a world? If so, which? If the world you are in isn't livable, then you are in a camp, outside of all worlds, where life has become unlivable. *Flow My Tears, the Policeman Said* is exemplary from this point of view. Its main character is a pure product of these artificial worlds: a famous public personality, a successful television host and singer, he lives in a world where political rivals are sent to work camps, where Black people are victims of a eugenics movement, and where students and professors live clandestinely in underground university campuses. The character is completely indifferent to the many kinds of violence perpetrated by this police state—up until the day he wakes up in a world in which he has never existed. It is the same world as before, except that he has never been a part of it. He is no longer anyone at all, he has no personal records and no identity. His friends, his lover, his manager, no one remembers him. "I am what they call an *unperson*" (685). *Deprived of all rights*, he now directly experiences a reality that "his" world's appearances had, up to that point, concealed from him. He discovers exclusion. "We have a betrayal state, he realized. When I was a celebrity I was exempt. Now I'm like everyone else: I now have to face what they've always faced. And—what I faced in the old days, faced and then later on repressed from my memory. Because it was too distressing to believe . . . once I had a choice, and could choose not to believe" (730).

8

THE DIGITAL HUMAN

(OR, WHAT IS AN ANDROID?)

In a universe in which the false finds its way into everything, where nothing escapes being contaminated by it, there will clearly also be false humans. "Fake realities will create fake humans."[1] This is a recurring character in SF, from the automaton and the robot to the android and the clone. Numerous SF films from the 1950s and '60s presented stereotypical scenes like the following: we're in a small, sleepy town with its shops, its police station, and its gas station, and the locals are all played by strangely inexpressive actors. They aren't bad actors, their characters' depth is just limited by their function: they are specimens or clichés. We know nothing of their personal lives or the states of their souls, and the small town in which they find themselves is completely isolated, cut off from everything. There is no world outside the scene of the action, no internal life independent of the action. But, because these characters are so lifeless and perfectly interchangeable, they really have no reality at all—and so can be vampirized, manipulated, and cloned. They even give the impression that it couldn't be otherwise, that they're only there for that reason. That may be the source of the success of Don Siegel's *Invasion of the Body Snatchers* (1956), whose characters grow inexpressive as they become inhuman and without anything having changed in their appearances. The model is the empty, inhuman individual, programmed and controlled. The danger is that your neighbor, friend, or parent could become a false human: the great American paranoia, illustrated by the McCarthy-era doctrine of the "enemy within," combines with the fear of an anonymization through proletarianization, the loss of bourgeois individual distinction for the sake of collective interest: communism as the ultimate alienation.

In Dick, false humans first appear in a classic guise: humans who are controlled by extraterrestrials, or sometimes aliens replacing humans through mimetic imitation, as in the story "The Father-Thing," where the son doubts that the man he is with is his real father and discovers alien larvae in the garden planning to replace his entire family.[2] Dick will repeatedly come back to the theme of alien invaders whose mimetic abilities allow them to take on a human form.[3] We aren't far from the particular paranoid delirium known as Capgras syndrome, which consists in believing that the people close to you have been replaced by imposters.

But Dick quickly realizes that it isn't useful to make the danger come from the depths of space. Humans dehumanize themselves all on their own; they willingly transform themselves into androids. This theme is just as conventional and classic: what threatens the humanity of human beings most is that they will be transformed into machines the moment machines themselves become "intelligent" and are "humanized."[4] For, as we know, the new cybernetic machines from the 1950s have acquired a kind of autonomy that makes them capable of modifying their behavior in relation to the information received. They record and transmit information, they communicate; in short, they are "humanized." This is the case with the famous door in *Ubik*, which refuses to open as long as the tenant hasn't paid his rent, and also with the drone in *Lies, Inc.*, which follows an individual down the street and berates him over a loudspeaker, telling him to pay his debts. It is the case with all the intelligent objects in Dick: doors, cars, coffee makers, beds. ("'You weigh one hundred and forty pounds,' the bed said. 'And there is exactly that weight extended over me. Therefore you are not engaged in copulation.'")[5]

If intelligent machines have taken over in Dick, it isn't because they have taken power but because they never stop offering "services," even and especially when those services don't serve any useful purpose.[6] Dick saw clearly that we had entered into a service society and that that implied a "growing domination of machines over man, especially the machines we voluntarily surround ourselves with, which should, by logic, be the most harmless. I never assumed that some huge clanking monster would stride down Fifth Avenue, devouring New York; I always feared that my own TV set or iron or toaster would, in the privacy of my apartment, when no one else was around to help me, announce to me that they had taken over, and here was a list of rules I was to obey."[7] We sign the service society's contract with our closed eyes: we will provide a service for you, but you will accept our conditions and follow all of our instructions. Service becomes a new form of enslavement. The process of substitution has been generalized; the toaster was just a modest first step. In Dick, all service activities will henceforth be handled by machines: cashiers, shopkeepers, taxicab drivers, doctors, surgeons, police officers, but also professors, the president of the United States, psychoanalysts (like the suitcase with a built-in psychiatrist in *The Three Stigmata of Palmer Eldritch*), and pets. In the Martian colonies, migrants can even "buy neighbors, buy the simulated presence of life, the sound and motion of human activity [. . .]. Therapeutically, this was helpful, although from a cultural standpoint it was a trifle sterile" (*The Simulacra*, 55–56).[8]

That services constitute a new form of enslavement is illustrated in the story "Sales Pitch," when the handyman robot declares: "You'll feel better after you've turned responsibility over to me" (S3, 221). While machines clearly do relieve people of the weight of certain tasks and responsibilities, they also impose new norms of behavior and thought upon them in doing so. There is a second phrase that complements the first, a phrase that the robot refrains from saying, which points to the irreversibility of technical "progress": "Once you have chosen me, you no longer have a choice." The individual willingly relinquishes her humanity to the benefit of the machines that complete her tasks better than she could and supposedly in a more humane way. That is the claim that lies at the heart of the new machines: we do everything better than humans do (memory, calculation, precision, decision, etc.). We are the new image of humanity, the image of the humanity to come. We are the purely rational, infallible, untiring human that is plugged straight into the grid: your greatest allies against the disorder of entropy, as Wiener said. At your service.

What is most unsettling, for Dick, is that people allow themselves to be seduced by the many offers of perfected services, and that these automatizations take over and hand us "a list of rules [we are] to obey" from then on. Power hasn't disappeared but has passed entirely into an anonymous and impersonal program, a depository of improved technical, social, moral, and therapeutic norms. "In this mode of domination, which proceeds by converting its orders into programs and its agents into automata, the power, already set at a distance, renders itself impossible to seize upon."[9] It tends to be confused with a purely automated operation, a self-regulated system of anonymous decision-making, from which all responsibility has disappeared, as much on the side of the users as on that of the designers and decision-makers.[10] *"You'll feel better after you've turned responsibility over to me."*

Dick often pushes this humanization of machines and androidization of humans to the point of rendering humans and machines indistinguishable. For instance, in "Second Variety," on a planet devastated by a war between the United States and the Soviet Union, machines, which have become autonomous and capable of auto-reproduction and invention, create new weapons designed to destroy the last remaining human soldiers.[11] They devise two models, first "the Wounded Soldier," then the abandoned child ("David and his bear"), meant to trick the soldiers by eliciting their sympathy. "One [of these Davids] gets in and it's all over [. . .]. One lets all the rest inside. They're inflexible. Machines with one purpose. They were built for only one thing" (S2, 41). As soon as it becomes possible to produce "false" humans, we end up in a situation where humans and machines, however distinct they may be, become externally indiscernible. That's what happens in the story: the humans kill their own, thinking they are destroying machines, and spare robots, believing they have saved humans.

In the novel *We Can Build You*, Dick pushes this indiscernibility even further, or rather, pushes it to the point of inversion: the machine becomes as human as the humans, while the humans become as in-human as machines. On the one hand, there is a business that decides to manufacture android prototypes, most notably an Abraham Lincoln, a perfect replica of the historical figure. The replica is so successful that it emanates a goodness, a vulnerability, "something innately good and warm and human."[12] On the other hand, the humans are cold and indifferent, like the young schizophrenic, the eternal "dark-haired girl" found in many of Dick's stories,[13] or the billionaire businessman who wants to manufacture androids on a massive scale and send them to the lunar colonies. "It was as if the brain part of Barrows, the shaved dome of his skull, had been lopped off and then skillfully replaced with some servo-system or some feedback circuit of solenoids and relays, all of which was operated from a distance off. Or operated by Something which sat upstairs there at the controls, pawing at the switches with tiny trick convulsive motions" (*We Can Build You*, 28–29). The method is simple enough: it isn't a matter of tricking humans but of revealing the fact that some humans are in fact inhuman.[14] We have passed over to the other side, from the "humanization" of machines to the androi-dization of humanity, which is encouraged by the image of the "new man" that workings of the cybernetic machines sketch out.

But then how do we recognize a human? Dick often poses this question and his answer is always the same: the characteristic mark of a human's humanity is empathy (*agape* or *caritas*, he doesn't distinguish between the two). The human is not a rational or thinking animal, but first and foremost an animal that sympathizes, that loves. This doesn't mean that we need to oppose empathy and intelligence, on the contrary.

"Maybe *caritas* is a factor of intelligence [. . .]. Maybe we've always been wrong: *caritas* is not a feeling but a high form of cerebral activity, an ability to perceive something in the environment—to notice and [. . .] to worry. Cognition [. . .]; that's what it is. It isn't a case of feeling versus thinking: cognition is cognition" (*Galactic Pot-Healer*, 109). The human is defined by her feeling of humanity. One might, like Fredric Jameson, deem this to be a "pop-psychological or pop-psychoanalytic notion" and a "vacuous theme."[15] It is true that empathy is a rather vague notion in Dick, sometimes taking the somewhat ridiculous form of an "empathy box" that allows people to participate in the Passion of a televised Christ, sometimes defined summarily as "the esteem of good people for one another,"[16] and sometimes considered to be the most important thing in the world, the only thing capable of saving us.

If Dick insists upon this notion to such a great extent, it isn't only because it relates back to the goodness of humanity or to humanist values, but because it is the thing in us that resists the generalized programming to which we are otherwise subjected. Everything unfolds as if the cerebral hemispheres were fighting against one another. The problem with the "digital," left hemisphere is its aptitude for working with algorithms and codes, and for allowing itself to be controlled by them to the point even of accepting their actual implementation. For Dick, the left hemisphere is dedicated to *the programming of the psyche*. The brain literally becomes a servo-mechanism; it adapts its own plasticity to conform to the alternatives preestablished by linguistic and numeric algorithms. "The basic tool for the manipulation of reality is the manipulation of words. If you can control the meaning of words, you can control the people who must use the words."[17]

On this point, Dick is rather close to William S. Burroughs, for whom the words of a language are tools used for taking control of brains and taking over their ability to construct realities. For Burroughs, the human brain is infected by a virus that spreads by means of language, its carrier. "Word begets image and image *is* virus."[18] Humanity is infected by its own "deteriorated image," as if it loved the idealized image of its inhumanity more than it loved itself. "So every species has a Master Virus: Deteriorated Image of that species. [. . .] The broken image of Man moves in minute by minute and cell by cell . . . Poverty, hatred, war, police-criminals, bureaucracy, insanity, all symptoms of The Human Virus."[19]

This proximity between Dick and Burroughs stems in part from their readings of Alfred Korzybski, whose work describes the way in which the use of language blocks the creativity born of relations found at the level of nonverbal experiences.[20] The structure of language tacitly imposes the rules of the old, bivalent, Aristotelian logic upon the "analogical" relations of the right hemisphere. If we need to be wary of language, it is because its logic exerts a control over our thoughts and because the images it gives rise to enclose our minds in an abstract world. From this point of view, "intelligent" machines participate in the spread of the virus. The spread of the social image of a rational, efficient, and emotionless human being and the promotion of this image by intelligent machines are two aspects of the same movement.

Fredric Jameson puts forward the hypothesis that SF came into being at the time when the great political utopias had begun to disappear from the social horizon.[21] But how can we fail to see the appearance, at the very moment when Dick began writing his first novels, of new sociopolitical utopias, which went hand in hand with developments in cybernetics and a renewed belief in "progress" stemming from the capacities of the new "intelligent" machines? These machines will replace the faulty humans whose behavior was revealed to be particularly irrational following the economic crises of the 1930s and during the Second World War.

The best way to ward off this irrationality would be to devise automated, rational systems whose very design would render irrationality definitively impossible—as if the Second World War hadn't already demonstrated the horrors of rationality itself. We need to develop machines capable of exceeding human capacities in crucial domains like decision-making and the execution of tasks. These machines will allow humans to adjust to their tasks better and will give them greater control over their activities, allowing them to adapt more successfully to the new situation that they themselves have created. "We have modified our environment so radically that we must now modify ourselves in order to exist in this new environment."[22] Hence the need to take control of psyches, to hypertrophy the left hemisphere, and to promote new human-machine complexes. To adapt to its new environment, a human doesn't need to be a living being anymore; it should become an android.[23] We can see why Simondon says that "the man who wants to dominate his peers calls the android machine into being."[24]

From the hopes kindled by the meetings of the Macy Conferences—where mathematicians, engineers, psychologists, anthropologists, logicians, and psychiatrists gathered with the goal of establishing a general science of the workings of the mind, but also of devising "thinking machines"—by way of Wiener's writings and the more recent futurological visions of thinkers like Jeremy Rifkin (among many others), utopia has rapidly transformed into a multitude of actual research programs.[25] To be sure, the term "utopia" doesn't quite fit here, if it is meant to designate something like a "no-place" or a nonsite. In the present case, the sites were several: States, military powers, secret services, "military-industrial" complexes, engineers, technological institutes, and universities (including departments of the human sciences) all invested in these programs of research and experimentation. We can't say that the sites were lacking; soon, the invasion would be total. No longer a utopia but a pantopia.

The new linguistics of generative grammar and the new cognitive psychology provide these programs with their new syntax and constitute a new "science of the mind." We have entered into the age of the new machines. Not only does the individual never leave her world, but she forces everything else she can into it by means of linguistic translation, informational coding, and digital conversion. "I think as I talk [. . .]; I am not a person but a self-admonishing voice. Worse, I talk as I hear. Garbage in (as the computer science majors say); garbage out" (*The Transmigration of Timothy Archer*, 622). The android is anyone who submits all of her perceptions to the hierarchies of her programming. Her brain has become a read head. "Programmed. In me somewhere [. . .] there is a matrix fitted in place, a grid screen that cuts me off from certain thoughts, certain actions. And forces me into others" (S5, 278–79).

The android's "intelligence" is devoid of intuition, or, what amounts to the same thing, its intuitions and emotions are limited entirely to what they can offer to its intelligence, which is itself subjected to an imperious will that surpasses it.[26] "The really inhuman person for our culture is the overtrained cerebral person."[27] If computers can take control of brains, it is because of the affinity they have with the "digital," left hemisphere. There is something like a vampirism inherent in computer surveillance, which absorbs life from those whose data it captures. "Once more, Nick gazed into the huge grotto-like chamber of the ten thousand TV screens. [. . .] He saw them as ectoplasmic spirits, without real bodies. These police coming and going on their errands; they had given up life a long time ago, and now, instead of living, they absorbed vitality from the screens which they monitored—or, more precisely, from the people on the screens" (*Our Friends from Frolix 8*, 101).

Empathy, on the other hand, which Dick sometimes lumps together with sympathy or compassion, is what allows one to *circulate between worlds*. Despite the profound difference between worlds, communication can be established between them through participation in an underlying common ground composed of movements that are paralinguistic, kinaesthetic, nonverbal, affective, emotional, pulsional, and so on. This communication doesn't result from digital translation but from analogical participation. It is musical, rhythmic, or silent, rather than linguistic. It isn't enclosed within a world but instead opens out onto other worlds and other forms of life. There is something ecological and cosmological about such communication, which points toward a profound vitalism.[28] Shifting the analogical/digital duality, we could say that the analogical circulates between worlds, while the digital is enclosed in a single because of the translational power of its codes.

In his own way, Dick rediscovers the distinction between cooperatives and bureaucracies that Burroughs established in *Naked Lunch*.

The former are founded upon the cooperation of individuals and their ability to share common realities, while the latter require a parasitic extraction to feed on. They never create anything of their own but must graft themselves onto existing activities and claim a share for themselves, in the manner of a tapeworm. "Bureaus cannot live without a host, being true parasitic organisms." While cooperatives function through "the building up of independent units to meet the needs of the people who participate in the functioning of the unit," bureaucracy must constantly invent new needs that justify its own existence.[29] It creates lacks that it justifies through the closed circuit of its redundancies. To put it in Dickian terms, bureaucracies can only live by grafting themselves onto existing worlds, which they subsume with their univocal, "digital" translations, while cooperatives find a common accord that allows for the continued existence of a plurality of worlds. It is as if the left hemisphere was bureaucratic and the right hemisphere cooperative.

The question therefore becomes: how do we promote the abilities of the right hemisphere? If Dick privileges music, it is because it constitutes an antilanguage or a subliminal language that activates zones of the brain different than those activated by linguistic communication. Music is inseparable from the sort of utopia of the subliminal that is so central to *Radio Free Albemuth*, but that can often be found in Dick's works whenever communication follows paths that are more subterranean than those of digital algorithms.[30] These paths are "analogical" forms of relation that travel from psyche to psyche, of which telepathy is a modality often seen in SF, even if Dick is a bit circumspect on that subject.[31] If telepathy intrudes into psyches to know their thoughts and strip them of their private lives (the horror of conjugality for Dick), it is also a way of entering into contact with the most profound levels of another psyche on a subliminal, molecular plane, following a model that owes much to the understanding of unconscious communication found in Jung. This is the level on which the force of love operates, where it rises up to the absolute and becomes an ultimate reality, beyond the relativizations of the intellect.[32] Empathy has a political force that acts through subreption, clandestine communication, subliminal messages, et cetera.

This is certainly why Dick grants so much importance to religion, as numerous texts from *The Exegesis* attest (some of which are returned to in the appendix of *VALIS*). Religion becomes the world of *caritas*, bearer of a "living information" that is addressed to the depths of the psyche. On the scale of world history, Dionysus, Brahma, Christ and his Apostles, Asclepius, and Zoroaster appear as so many subliminal emissaries destined to overturn the "Empire," whose reign has continued from Rome to the present day. In *The Exegesis*, Dick often compares the United States of 1974 to a metal prison that he calls the Empire or the BIP (Black Iron Prison) and understands to be a prolongation of the Roman Empire from the first centuries.[33] What has made the continuity of the empire through the centuries possible is the Sibyl, the guardian of the Roman republic. "Since she was immortal she had continued on after Rome vanished . . . vanished but still existent in new forms, with new linguistic systems and new customs. But the heart of the Empire remained [. . .]. After the Dark Ages we had built back up to what had been and even more. The prongs of imperialism had been extended all the way to Southeast Asia."[34]

But religions obey a different temporality, possess a different memory, and transmit different messages. They are political forces of the future and are alone capable of freeing us from this millenary conditioning. This time, the distinction between the hemispheres signals an ancestral battle between two all-powerful entities. On the one hand, the Empire, the malady of the Earth, which spreads like a virus; on the other, the emissaries of living information, the doctors who appear sporadically over the course of history to free humanity from its mental conditioning. They address themselves to the ancestral memories buried in the collective unconscious, to the "memory banks" deposited in us; they try to stimulate them through secret signals that act as "deconditioning instructions" according to a high-tech version of the historial.[35]

Generally speaking, the notebooks that were feverishly written during an eight-year period following the "religious experiences" of February–March 1974 and brought together under the title *The Exegesis* are a testament to the encounter that took place between the deliria of religion, Dick's own deliria, and his inventiveness in the domain of science fiction. His "exegetic" work does not consist in a return to the "letter" of the sacred texts but rather in a phantasmatic and delirious compilation of hypotheses coming from a wide variety of sources. We aren't far from the exegeses inspired by the *scientia Dei*, which, when they "glossed the Annunciation, they saw in it something like a crystalline unique event, and at the same time they saw in it an absolutely extravagant efflorescence of inclusive or associated meanings, of virtual connections, of memories, of prophecies touching upon everything, from the creation of Adam to the end of time, from the simple form of the letter M (the initial of Mary) to the prodigious construction of angelic hierarchies."[36]

We find the same proliferation in Dick, with the difference that his exegesis is just as likely to evoke the Cumaean Sibyl as Asclepius the healer, Osiris as Dionysus, or Brahma and Vishnu, or Akhenaten and Shiva, or the *I Ching*—but also information theory, the *Bardo Thodol*, references to Plato, Hegel, the *Tao Te Ching*, Whitehead, Jung, and Giordano Bruno, not to mention elements of *Gestalttheorie*, texts from the occultist tradition (which are a sort of proto-SF), and esoteric writings like those of the strange, controversial archaeologist John Allegro, who believed that the relation to God in primitive Christianity was tied to the ritual consumption of hallucinogenic mushrooms.[37] All of these accumulated readings have the sole objective of resolving the enigma of the religious crisis of "February–March 1974" from a perspective that is at once clinical, metaphysical, metapsychological, cosmological, theological, and ontological. "I can see myself telling my therapist this. 'What's on your mind, Phil?' she'll say when I go in, and I'll say, 'Asklepios is my tutor, from out of Periclean Athens. I'm learning to talk in Attic Greek.' She'll say, 'Oh really?' and I'll be on my way to [. . .] the country where it's quiet and costs $100 a day. And you get all the apple juice you want to drink, along with Thorazine."[38]

Has he gone so far as to believe that his novels are really holy books, dictated by a divine power? "As I keep saying, I feel retrospectively that *Tears* and very likely *Frolix 8* were both engineered subliminally, carrying in encoded or stegenographic form material from the Logos or Godhead concerning the Logos or Godhead" (*Exegesis*, 185–86). Which is to say, a book like *Ubik* wouldn't have been written by Dick, but by Ubik itself, the divinity that is present in the story under various forms, "which makes the novel a form of scripture" (*Exegesis*, 299). Isn't everything he wrote a foreshadowing of his religious experiences: the plurality of worlds, the clash of divinities, the "false" worlds, the proliferation of information, sometimes deceptive, sometimes redeeming? "One could regard my 27 years of writing as a kind of apprenticeship, leading up to the moment when I would be ready for the 2-3-74 experience" (*Exegesis*, 301). He comes to describe his life "before" the way psychiatrists of the nineteenth century described the incubation phase that precedes psychotic episodes.[39] All of his novels become premonitory tales and make Dick into a sort of "precog" of himself.

If the *Exegesis* sometimes gives the impression that Dick is "lost" for SF and that he has passed over into a form of religious esotericism, the novels that are contemporary with this period indicate that the contrary is, in fact, the case: in them, it is the religious content that has passed entirely over into SF. In *VALIS*, Christ becomes an electromagnetic transmitter, God becomes an extraterrestrial station that the Russians are trying to destroy, the world has become a hologram that a divinity projects in order to exploit us, and so forth. It is through his paranoid and megalomaniacal deliria that Dick was able to confront religious deliria, which are perhaps SF greatest rival but also a valuable ally. Was religion not the first to create delirious worlds, similar to those of SF, with its miracles, its supernatural interventions, and its superterrestrial beings, gods, angels, seraphim, and spirits? Didn't it hope to welcome all the abnormal psychic states, deliria, trances, visions, and hallucinations into its heart, to make them signs of the other world? It was therefore normal for Dick, in the grip of delirium, to turn to religion finally to reincorporate its deliria into the field of SF. If it can be said of Philip K. Dick that he "completed" SF, it is less because he exhausted the genre—exploring both the genre and the parody of the genre—than because he revealed the religious or mythological temptation that perhaps lies dormant in the foundations of every SF story.

What characterizes all of these deliria is not that hallucinations or "subjective" visions are taken to be real but rather that *they make it possible to take false worlds to be unreal*. According to Louis A. Sass, schizophrenic deliria are not characterized by the confusion of the real and the imaginary or by the regression toward an archaic world, as Dick thought, based on his readings of Jung and Freud, but by the conviction that everything the world takes to be true or "objectively real" is in fact shot through with irreality.[40] If dualism is a recurring form in Dick's oeuvre—particularly following his religious experiences—sometimes borrowing from Platonism, sometimes from the Gnostics (Prison versus Palmeraie, disorder versus information, destructive morbidity versus creative vitality, etc.); it isn't because it allows him to assert the reality of an afterworld but, on the contrary, because it allows him to discredit the counterfeit reality of the world in which we are forced to live, to make it into a "false" world that directs our attention away from the reality of the world. But how do we continue to believe in this world without accepting the falsifications that are imposed on us? Which fictions, which realities can be invented that will allow us to escape from the "false" world and to transform it without falling back into a fiction of afterworlds?[41] "Any system which says, This is a rotten world, wait for the next, give up, do nothing, succumb—that may be the basic Lie" (*Exegesis*, 19).

9

We have distinguished two kinds of character in Dick: on the one hand, the androids, the programmed humans who allow nothing to distract them from the goals they pursue. Their entire being is dominated by a fixed idea. They expend their energy only in the service of this idea, making them similar to machines—or to insects, following a recurring image in Dick. Their ultimate goal is the possession or preservation of a world, of "their" world. They only know how to command and execute, the two operations found in all programming. On the other hand, there are the individuals who try to escape from these worlds, adhering to various forms of sympathy, from compassion to empathy, from *agape* to *caritas*. Instead of being enclosed in a world, they circulate between worlds, at the risk of foundering in madness or being taken in by the "empathy box" that leaves them no other choice than to identify with a televised Christ.

With the paranoids, we have seen that this fixed idea is full of hate, that it is profoundly hateful, and that, when followed to the end, it leads to the destruction of every form of life. We even find a comical scientist who believes that the origin of life is pure resentment, proceeding from a Principle of Sufficient Irritation: "Eons ago, in the remote past, a bit of inanimate matter had become so irritated by something that it crawled away, moved by indignation" (S1, 300). This confirms that, for the paranoid, everything is purely reaction: everything that comes from without attacks, irritates, and provokes him, even when he is alone. There is something unbearable in the very fact of living. "This must be the neurological spring that sets psychotic paranoia going, he reflected. The acute unpleasant awareness of being watched. [. . .] Even the fear component was minor; the sense of conspicuousness itself was the overwhelming factor, the unbearable part" (*The Penultimate Truth*, 75). Hence this inflexible will, destined to hate every form of life.

In many respects, Dick agrees with Lawrence's diagnosis:

> Everything in America goes by *will*. A great negative *will* seems to be turned against all spontaneous life—there seems to be no *feeling* at all—no genuine bowels of compassion and sympathy, all this gripped, iron, and *benevolent* will, which in the end is diabolic. [. . .] And that's why I think America is neither free nor brave, but a land of tight, iron-clanking little *wills,* everybody trying to put it over everybody else, and a land of men absolutely devoid of the real courage of trust, trust in life's sacred spontaneity. They can't trust life until they can *control* it.[1]

The willful beings in Dick are driven by a fixed idea or an "over-va-lent" idea to which they are slaves.[2] It isn't servo-mechanism anymore, but servo-ideism or servo-idealism. We can't even really say that this will belongs to them, so much are they subjected to it. Even when they are in command, they have a profound taste for obedience, the obedience of others as much as their own.[3] The will is another name for the faculty of obeying and making others obey. "Becoming what I call, for lack of a better term, an android, means, as I said, to allow oneself to become a means, or to be pounded down, manipulated, made into a means without one's knowledge or consent—the results are the same. [. . .] Androidization requires obedience."[4]

Everything is fixed for the Dickian paranoid, not just her system of thought but also her face, an inexpressive mask, which has become a simple camera or one-way mirror.

> Paranoid eyes. [. . .] This was not the glittering, restless stare of ordinary suspicion; this was a motionless gaze, a gathering of the totality of faculties within to comprise a single undisturbed psychomotor concentration. [. . .] He was helpless, compelled to confront his compatriots and adversaries alike in this fashion, with this unending ensnaring fixity. It was an attentiveness which made empathic understanding impossible; the eyes did not reflect any inner reality; they gave back to the viewer exactly what he himself was. The eyes stopped communication dead; they were a barrier that could not be penetrated this side of the tomb. (*Now Wait for Last Year*, 569)

The paranoid is one of those cold and calculating characters whose faces are no more than masks. It is as if, having too much to hide, they stayed hidden *behind* their faces, making it necessary to break through them, like shells, to reveal the inner faces that they had been concealing.[5] But there are also paranoid characters who display a completely different kind of behavior: those who multiply their mimicry and project themselves *in front of* their faces, making them disappear behind an overacted expressivity, a forced spontaneity, hoping to hide the extent to which their faces nevertheless betray them. "I am warm on the outside, what people see. Warm eyes, warm face, warm fucking fake smile, but inside I am cold all the time, and full of lies" (*A Scanner Darkly*, 1081).

If there are so many paranoids in Dick's works, that is due, first and foremost, to the climate of paranoia that took hold during the Cold War, from McCarthyism to Watergate, though also to the social changes that came with it. In his own way, Dick anticipates the analyses of Stuart Ewen, according to whom the invasion of advertising encouraged paranoia in the construction of the self.[6] Don't you have a bad complexion? What do you look like with your outmoded style? Aren't you out of touch? Advertisements in Dick are often of this kind, whether encouraging paranoia ("Defend your privacy, the ads yammered on the hour, from all media. Is a stranger tuning in on you? Are you *really* alone? [. . .] Are your actions being predicted by someone you never met?" [*Ubik*, 616]) or provoking it directly, as with the psychotic pianist in *The Simulacra*, who, because of an advertisement for perfume, has "acquired a phobic body odor" and is convinced he could contaminate the entire world (*The Simulacra*, 60).

Another characteristic of the paranoid is the impossibility of him ever leaving "his" world, since he must constantly defend it against the threat of invasion. How could he renounce the delirious axiom that directs his entire system of thought, when this axiom constrains him to be vigilant at every moment and to survey the boundaries of his world constantly to protect it from even the slightest intrusion?[7] His ideas are fixed in the sense that they literally bind the individual to his world. Not only is the paranoid necessarily alone, but he tries to isolate others, to engender in them the same circle of mistrust as the one by which he is surrounded. His solitude is not populated; it is necessarily unpopulated, because the appearance of anyone else would threaten the total control he otherwise exercises in "his" world. He is an agent of atomization in the image of the great paranoid who wants to detonate bombs of more and more devastating magnitudes.[8] *We must atomize everything*, matter as well as the social sphere, so that everyone will find herself politically and socially alone (against everyone else). Individualism—in all of its forms—is first of all a paranoid thought. The enemy is *the liaison* between atoms or individuals, it is any form of collaboration, cooperation, et cetera. "Facing Freneksy, they became as they were born: isolated and individual, unsupported by the institutions which they were supposed to represent. [. . .] The normal *relativeness* of existence, lived with others in a fluctuating state of more or less adequate security, had vanished. [. . .] Casting his principle over the conference room and the people in it, as if forcing everyone away from each other step by step" (*Now Wait for Last Year*, 570; 573).

Beyond the generalized mistrust and total lack of empathy, what interests Dick is the paranoid's aptitude for reasoning on the basis of "false postulates from which he has relentlessly constructed an elaborate system of beliefs, logical and consistent with these false postulates."[9] The paranoid's system of thought is presented as an arrangement of barricades, making thought into an act of self-defense.[10] What are these false postulates? They could be formulated as follows: the more appearances seem to go against you, the more justified you are, because the fundamental principle is that you should never trust in appearances. In other words, as long as the "virus of righteousness" remains virulent within her, the paranoid is always right.[11] In this sense, the paranoid is really a person with a single idea that acts with the force of a final principle, not because it is the most elevated principle but because it is the last one remaining. This axiom is the last of the unconditionally true ideas, the only one to have survived all of the critiques and all of the destruction that the paranoid has been able to unleash in its name.

The story that best illustrates this description is "Shell Game," one of Dick's masterpieces, which tells the story of a ship that is stranded on an alien planet, whose crew is convinced that an elusive, unknown enemy is attempting to eliminate them by any number of different means: odorless gas, poisoned water, the spread of viruses and bacterial residues, not to mention the possibility of an enemy spy having infiltrated the group. A member of the crew discovers an audio recording from which they learn that they are actually paranoid mental patients on board a hospital-ship. "What are we to believe? *Are there any attackers?*" (S3, 235). To solve their dilemma, they decide to subject themselves to a collective test. But the situation quickly degenerates as a result of the test; they end up killing one another because one member of the crew senses that the whole story of the recording and the test is just a trap designed to get rid of them. It's all there: the mistrust, the destructive hatred, and the fixed idea. "The tapes point out how tenacious paranoids are. They cling fanatically to their fixed beliefs. [. . .] There'll be a fight and we might win because we're more one-track. We would never deviate" (S3, 239).

Through his critique of the fixed idea and the obsessive madness of the will, Dick situates himself within a long tradition of American literature. We are thinking, of course, of Ahab, the great obsessive, driven by a fixed idea of vengeance, and also of the splendid description of the Indian-hater's fixed idea in *The Confidence-Man*.[12] It was really Melville who showed the extent to which a fixed idea transforms an individual into an obsessive *hunter*. If this notion traverses American literature from the hunters of Native Americans and nonbelievers in the stories of James Fenimore Cooper and Nathaniel Hawthorne, and from the "Indian hunts" in Melville, to the android hunters of *Do Androids Dream of Electric Sheep?*, it is because the history of the United States unfolds as an uninterrupted succession of manhunts: hunting Native Americans, hunting Black people, hunting witches, hunting workers, immigrants, vagabonds, and communists. The lands of the "Frontier" weren't just thought of as a world to be conquered, but as the arena of a manhunt, Count Zaroff's Island expanded to the proportions of a continent.

This manhunt, always led by white people, viewed itself as a hunt for the inhuman, which it defined as what was other than the white man. It is always the other who is hunted. She isn't considered human but is seen as some sort of a "creature," who is under the control either of her instincts (human-beast, subhuman, inferior human), of diabolical forces (nonbeliever, Satanist), or of foreign powers (communist agent, machine-human). In all these cases, there's no longer anything human about her. All intruders are enemies and all enemies have something inhuman about them. That's why paranoids can see even objects become "malevolent" and turn into their enemies.[13] In the case of the hunt, it is no longer a question of an enemy; or rather, the enemy has become the game, *the most dangerous game.*

The other solution, which is really only a shameful complement of the first, no longer consists in unleashing a murderous will, but in an committing an act of charity—not Dickian *caritas* but a dehumanizing charity, the "diabolic," "iron, and benevolent will," of which Lawrence speaks. This charity is benevolent only in that it spares lives; sometimes it even assures them the minimal conditions necessary for survival. But, in reality, it is always a hunt, and in this case it is hunting the inhumans straight out of the world. No longer extermination but the interminable agony of camps, reservations, or ghettos. An inflexible *will* on the one hand, *charity* transformed into piety on the other, the two hemispheres having become the jaws of an inhuman vice.

In *Ronald Reagan, the Movie, and Other Episodes in Political Demonology*, Michael Rogin points out that prior to the War of Secession, the hunt focused on Native Americans and Black people in the South and the West. Later, the conflicts shifted to include urban zones and focus on the hunt of immigrant workers and unions (which doesn't prevent the old hunts from continuing, as well). With the Cold War, the enemy changes again. Now, it is the supposed agents of the Soviet Union that have become the enemy, an enemy that is more and more internal, more and more invisible and potentially anyone and anywhere, leading to a more and more paranoid State.[14] "The government began to hire and employ [. . .] agents out of uniform who went around and checked up on anyone suspected of being a threat to security, either for what he had once done, such as Nicholas, or what he was doing now, such as me, or for what he might do in the future, as was possible with all of us" (*Radio Free Albemuth*, 63). The exemplary figure of this paranoia, for Dick, isn't so much McCarthy as Nixon and his madness about espionage.

With the Cold War, not only does the enemy become invisible (now she might be as white as all the others), it is also impossible to tell her apart from the person chasing her, as in *Do Androids Dream of Electric Sheep?*, where the android hunter might be an android himself. Then, the predator becomes his own prey and begins to spy on himself. The narcotics agent in *A Scanner Darkly* keeps tabs on the dealer that he himself has become. The left hemisphere is the camera that spies on all the movements of the right hemisphere. We are on board the ship from "Shell Game," where everyone suspects everyone else. It is therefore also necessary to hunt thoughts, hence the telepathic police officers we find throughout Dick's works, as in the story "The Hood Maker" (S2). This means that the hunter can no longer have the same assurance as before, because the enemies have insinuated themselves into everything, even into our brains. To be sure, he hunts something that is other than human (the programmed, indoctrinated human-machine), but she can no longer know for sure if she herself is still human and if the other isn't more human than she is. That's the whole problem: what can assure her, during the hunt, that she is pursuing the right prey and that she herself hasn't become the very prey she is after? That is the question of the paranoid hunter. "Is a stranger tuning in on you? Are you *really* ever alone?"

10

BETWEEN LIFE AND DEATH

—You know, Crayne said, it's a hell of an experience to be dead.

—Speak for yourself.

PHILIP K. DICK, "A LITTLE SOMETHING

FOR US TEMPUNAUTS"

The general problem of Dick's work—what is reality?—is closely tied to another problem, which is just as crucial: what is living and what is dead? How do you distinguish between them? How do you know that you are alive and not dead? This question troubles many of Dick's characters: am I alive or am I dead? Androids aren't just robots that trick humans by imitating them, they are also humans who lack vitality and live a counterfeit life. If it is possible to be taken in by androids, that is because there are also devitalized humans among the living, "imitation" humans with what Winnicott calls a "false self." "Thanatos can assume any form it wishes; it can kill eros, the life drive, and then simulate it. Once thanatos does this to you, you are in big trouble; you suppose you are driven by eros but it is thanatos wearing a mask" (*VALIS*, 287), which is particularly the case with Dickian paranoiacs.

In Dick, the living are those who serve life; the dead, those who serve death, who subjugate and mutilate life. The absence of empathy in program-humans makes them people who are dead, who "can't trust life until they can control it," to use Lawrence's formulation. They are dead despite their being alive, despite their ability to perceive, and their faces are nothing more than masks that simulate emotion and affection. We can see why Burroughs speaks of a virus: something neither living nor dead has taken possession of the human brain, has separated humanity from its vitality, and has substituted for it an independent, artificial life that seeks to extend itself beyond all organic life.

We have seen that, in *A Scanner Darkly*, the main character undergoes a cerebral death, a death of his sensibility, which transforms him into a pure instrument of vision, a walking camera. The point isn't to depict addicts as zombies but to show how the character dies and yet organically survives this death, emptied of all substance: he is now just an eye past which images file by.[1] "Imagine being sentient but not alive. Seeing and even knowing, but not alive. Just looking out. Recognizing but not being alive. A person can die and still go on. Sometimes what looks out at you from a person's eyes maybe died back in childhood. What's dead in there still looks out. It's not just the body looking at you with nothing in it; there's still something in there but it died and just keeps on looking and looking; it can't stop looking" (*A Scanner Darkly*, 1069). The junky has become a camera without memory, a vacant eye.

Many of Dick's stories involve individuals who are dead on the inside even though they are still organically alive.[2] But what interests him most is the opposite: all those cases in which individuals who are organically dead nevertheless continue to live. In such cases, a new limit gets blurred: no longer between reality and illusion or self and nonself, but between *life and death*. The alternative—living or dead—can no longer be maintained. In Dick, one can be both at the same time or neither the one nor the other, neither completely dead nor completely alive. "Are we dead or aren't we? First you say one then, then you say another. Can't you be consistent?"[3] Being already dead while you are still alive or, conversely, making the dead into beings that still live. One of the most striking cases is the child in *Dr. Bloodmoney*, "whose brother lived inside her body, down in the inguinal region . . . no larger than a baby rabbit" (353). He can hear the voices of the dead, "those empty pooh-pooh dead that never have any fun or nothing," and complains about his fetal life to his sister (408). This larval brother is literally between life and death, allowing communication to take place between the two worlds.[4]

One characteristic shared by many of Dick's stories is that their characters are dead *from the beginning*. The opening lines of the story "Rautavaara's Case" are exemplary in this regard: "The three technicians of the floating globe monitored fluctuations in interstellar magnetic fields, and they did a good job up until the moment they died" (S5, 453). This immediately raises a question: if all the characters are dead as early as the first sentence, what's left for there to happen? How do they live if they're already dead? The same question arises with *Eye in the Sky*, in which all of the characters fall into a coma at the end of the second chapter, or with *Ubik*, whose protagonists are killed in an explosion at the start of the novel. This means that these stories tell the destinies of dead characters, of characters immersed in a "semi-living" state, as if the famous statement from Poe's story, "now—*I am dead*," had opened up new possibilities.[5] As Stanisław Lem says, the realist novel can't describe what happens to its heroes after they die; they have to end there, while SF is free to continue its tale.

Insofar as SF ceaselessly raises the question of survival, we can see why Dick would be interested in *postmortem* forms of life. How will you continue to live if you're going to be dead? This is an obsession with certain of Dick's characters, especially with many who hold political power, as if power were inseparable from a fantasy of immortality as the supreme fixed idea. This is the case with the hypochondriac dictator Molinari in *Now Wait for Last Year*, the secretary of the United Nations and "leader" of an Earth at war against alien invaders.[6] His condition hovers ever on the brink of death, forcing negotiations with the enemy to be constantly deferred. His endless agony constitutes a veritable "instrument of political strategy" (*Now Wait for Last Year*, 660), forcing him to contract—through empathy—any fatal illness from which a member of his team is suffering. "His hypochondria was real; he did not merely have hysterical symptoms—he had true diseases which usually turned the patient into a terminal case" (535). He is constantly on the verge of dying and sometimes he really does die; he even dies several times during a decisive meeting for the fate of the Earth. It is as if Molinari had to kill himself constantly to ensure political survival. And he succeeds by using the bodies of other Molinaris, taken from parallel worlds, that perish one after another like a cache of spare bodies. In this way, he establishes a new kind of dynasty, founded not upon diachrony but upon synchrony. He brings about what may ultimately be the secret dream of every dynasty: to succeed yourself into perpetuity.

It is like a new version of Kantorowicz's theory of the king's two bodies in the political theology of the Middle Ages. The sovereign was an exceptional being who brought together two bodies within himself: an organic, human body and a divine, political body. The natural body is a mortal body, subject to illness, wounds, and death, while the political body is a glorious, invisible, untouchable body that "is utterly void of Infancy, and old Age, and other natural Defects and Imbecilities," including death. Its members are not the same as those of the organic body but are the subjects of the kingdom, of which he is the "head" or "soul." This duality can be interpreted in two ways: either as a *dissociation* between the eternal, political body of the kingdom and the natural bodies that successively take the place of its "head" or, on the contrary, as a *gemination*. In the latter case, the sovereign, like Christ, would possess a double nature: mortal by nature and immortal by grace.[7]

Clearly, the problem isn't posed in the same terms in Dick's work. It is no longer theologico-political, but techno-political: for the God–human duality, he substitutes a human–machine duality. In the case of Molinari, the situation is reminiscent of the old process of gemination; only now that the resources of a transcendent world have become inaccessible, it is necessary to turn to parallel worlds. Lacking the effects of a higher grace and the performative virtues of theological dogma, all we have left to count on is drugs and medical technology. Hence, a body that is constantly patched back together by grafting synthetic organs onto it (the "artiforgs"). Resurrection is no longer a matter of grace but of transplantation.

The same is true of the phocomelus in *Dr. Bloodmoney,* one of Dick's most disturbing characters, somewhere between Richard III and Richard Nixon. Driven by a deep resentment, he substitutes for his underdeveloped body a technological one that he controls cerebrally with the help of paranormal powers. "I used to be body-wired. Now I'm brain-wired; I did that myself, too" (314). He swaps his organic body for an authoritarian body politic, thanks to which he is able to exert his domination over a small community of survivors following a nuclear war. As in the case of Molinari, this is no longer a question of a mystical body but of a technological body, controlled by paranormal mental powers. The character's transformation is accompanied by megalomaniacal deliria and prophetic visions of himself as the master of the world. He is one of those beings who entirely lack empathy and harbor a secret hatred of all life. And it is precisely this android part that seeks to survive and set itself free from all organic "support," so as to maintain its control over the others eternally.

That SF allows for a duality of bodies to be constituted by means of gemination does not mean that the hypothesis of a duality constituted by means of dissociation need therefore be abandoned. Only, it won't be a question of dissociating the eternal body of the kingdom from the natural bodies that successively take their place at its head; it is now a question of dissociating the real government from the images of consensus that it produces to perpetuate itself. This dissociation is above all a matter of images. On the one hand, images of power; on the other hand, a real power, but without images, as in *The Simulacra.* On the one hand, there are the immortal false images: that of an eternal president (who has really been replaced by an android) and that of Nicole Thibodeaux, the "First Lady," who is extremely popular on television (but who has really been dead for a long time and whose role has been played by actresses ever since).[8] Behind these false figures, there is a governmental council that has no legal existence and whose members are only visible "indirectly, through elaborate screening devices" (*The Simulacra*, 187). Dissociation has become dissimulation. Kings no longer succeed each other; now, artificial political figures, actors or robots, are created, as with the android president of *The Penultimate Truth*, whose speeches are written by a computer. "What entered Megavac 6-V as mere *logos* would emerge for the TV lenses and mikes to capture in the guise of a pronouncement, one which nobody in his right mind—would doubt" (*The Penultimate Truth*, 33). What's most important now isn't to ensure the survival of a providential man by all "geminative" means possible but to ensure the preservation of a deceptive popular image, which is dissociated from the very political program it perpetuates. The work of politics in the age of mechanical reproduction.

This can be seen again in the novella "What the Dead Men Say" (S4), which tells the story of an important businessman who wants to be revived just after his death to help get his preferred presidential candidate elected. Only, the attempts to reanimate him fail. His daughter is his only heir but is also a drug addict and a mystic. Inexplicably, the dead man is ultimately able to transmit messages from a distant satellite anyway, and his propagandistic messages overwhelm the media, allowing his otherwise mediocre candidate to take the election. It hardly matters when, in the end, we learn that this was really a strategy enacted by his daughter, who is capable of perfectly imitating her father's voice. This just means that the father has descended to inhabit his daughter, and that she has comprehended and incorporated him so well that she has become a sort of avatar, a semi-resurrection or an organic prolongment, a child-graft and a tool of political reproduction.[9] To each his own pseudo-dynasty.

The body politic has become an informational avatar. I die organically, but I survive informationally—there is no interruption of the program. Insert your brain into the machines, collaborate with them, become a machine yourself, transmit your information, your programs, your images and sounds. The show goes on because you have been recorded, you have become an audiovisual body with a new *cogito*. I film myself, I record myself, *ego video, ego audio*, like the agent in *A Scanner Darkly*. You turn yourself into an avatar made of images and sounds within a program and thereby become an agent of its propagation. This is another way for the left hemisphere to dominate the right hemisphere: by making it into a digitized avatar. The deceased absorbs the living person and her code. At the limit, each person creates her own double, her own avatar of images and sounds, and vampirizes herself. It all takes place like a transfer of vitality: all the information passes over to the avatar, while the real individual works constantly to supply more and more data. "Once more, Nick gazed into the huge grotto-like chamber of the ten thousand TV screens. [. . .] He saw them as ectoplasmic spirits, without real bodies. These police coming and going on their errands; they had given up life a long time ago, and now, instead of living, they absorbed vitality from the screens which they monitored—or, more precisely, from the people on the screens" (*Our Friends from Frolix 8*, 101).

In this respect, isn't Richard Nixon the Dickian antihero par excellence? A Christ figure turned on its head, taking on all of the negativity, absorbing all of the country's paranoia, and having two distinct bodies of his own: an organic body and a body of political paranoia, namely, the White House, filled with microphones to guarantee total control over the political realm. It isn't divine grace that now guarantees immortality but the innumerable hours of recordings. Michael Rogin shows that Nixon constituted a new body politic by equipping the White House with a generalized system of wiretapping.[10] This is the new body politic, with its microphones and its delirious paranoid brain, as dissociated from itself as the narcotics agent in *A Scanner Darkly*. How could Dick have failed to be fascinated by Nixon to the point of making him a character in a few of his novels (in *Radio Free Albemuth* and *VALIS*)?[11] And how could he not have interpreted the fall of Nixon as a good omen, since it meant that he was no longer the master of information?

It is no longer a matter of guaranteeing the eternity of a body but of perpetuating a program that allows one to control a world. The idea is to survive in the form of a program or code, to continue exerting control over the brains of others, like the young vampire in *Ubik*. Without a doubt, it is *Ubik* that, in the character Jory, most clearly sets forth the implications of the desire to survive in this manner. Like the story "Rautavaara's Case," *Ubik* follows a team of investigator-hunters, whose members all die at the very beginning of the story, the victims of an explosion. We therefore follow the fates of dead characters, in a delirious version of the *Bardo Thodol*, the *Tibetan Book of the Dead*. Everyone thinks that they have survived; none of them know that they have been placed in a "moratorium" and kept in a semi-live state. Little by little, they realize that they are moving through a strange world, subject to inexplicable transformations. On the one hand, time turns back on itself in an accelerated way: cream sours, coffee grows moldy, appliances and vehicles revert to older forms. On the other hand, the characters begin to die, one after another, victims of an accelerated process of aging, to the point of crumbling into dust, "almost mummified," in less than a single night.

Behind this world that has submitted to a runaway entropy, we discover a sort of vampire or parasite, young Jory, who has been placed in semi-life in the same moratorium as the others and who "eats" what remains of the lives of the other semi-live inhabitants in order to prolong his own existence. Jory acts like a virus that infects the worlds of the semi-living and absorbs their vital energy, hence their nearly instantaneous desiccation. As always in Dick, the war of the worlds is a war of the psyches. In this state of semi-life, the worlds have become virtual, while the psyches have become telecommunication devices. Brains are transmitters with which one can only communicate by tuning into the right frequency. With *Ubik*, we have definitively passed into a world where no one is alive anymore: all that remains are virtual worlds at war with one another, which only live by vampirizing the small amount of vital energy left for brains to feed on. Making the world that you have created survive at the cost of all others: that is the goal. And it is in this sense that the survival of a world requires a political body.

The human-machines, the semi-living, the androids, and all the other beings that are devoid of vitality are the agents of this parasitism, signs of an illness or a "breakdown" of our vital system. "We appear to be memory coils (DNA carriers capable of experience) in a computer-like thinking system which, although we have correctly recorded and stored thousands of years of experiential information, and each of us possesses somewhat different deposits from all the other life forms, there is a malfunction—a failure—of memory retrieval. There lies the trouble in our particular subcircuit" (*VALIS*, 259).

11

BRICOLAGE (OR, THE RANDOM VARIABLE)

Henry James distinguished novelists on the basis of a time of day or a light that was properly their own, "the color of the air" with which the novelist suffuses his or her novel: the morning light in Dickens or the waning late-afternoon light in George Eliot, the endless autumn of Charlotte Brontë or the arrested spring of Jane Austen.[1] This characteristic hour determines the temporal structure of the stories; it determines their mode of temporalization. What James doesn't say, but which his discussion implies, is that it is also a manner of situating oneself in relation to the central event that organizes the story. From which temporal dimension is it grasped? Upon which immobile hour does the novelist perch in order to observe the passage of time? Is it at the very beginning or at the point when things start to pick up again? Or is it when everything is drawing to a close, or falling apart? Or is it at twilight, when we don't yet understand what is about to happen? Or perhaps when nothing ever happens, or nearly so? For, clearly a novelist's propitious hour is inseparable from her way of making us perceive events and of situating us with respect to them.

Of SF as a genre, we can say with Lem that it begins in the time *after*.[2] The story begins after a catastrophe, which is to say, after the catastrophe that has created the situation in which the story begins. War, epidemic, alien invasion, cataclysm, nuclear explosion, and so on: SF explores all of the catastrophic possibilities in order to describe what happens in the time after. We are in the future, but in a future that has broken with our present and is therefore a time posterior to human history. Dick does not depart from this rule: his stories often begin after devastating wars that have rendered the Earth uninhabitable and led to the colonization of other planets. If the atmosphere of the Cold War permeates them, it isn't just because his stories echo the profound paranoia of the United States but because this war brings with it the virtual destruction of the world and the end of humanity.

Thus, many of his stories begin after a third world war in which the confrontation of two blocs leads to their mutual annihilation. For him, this situation is simply a given, it is merely a backdrop or an exterior setting. Dick often describes isolated human communities, sometimes people banished to colonies on a hostile planet or aboard a ship lost in space, sometimes groups of survivors starting over from scratch after a devastating war. And another sign of the Cold War is Dick's predilection for populations living underground to shelter themselves from radiation, who become as pale as earthworms and sometimes even lose their eyesight, having no use for it anymore anyway.[3]

What is essential is not only what happens afterward but the deflagration it causes in people's psyches, as if their brains had also exploded or, worse, as if their brains had been the cause of the explosion. Dick almost never describes the catastrophe itself, since his stories begin after it has already taken place. Jameson rightly points out that one of the rare atomic explosions described by Dick—in *Dr. Blood-money*—is caused by the violent psychic implosion of one of the book's characters (who thinks he just has a severe inner-ear problem).[4] The explosion is literally triggered by his cerebral activity, making it an event that is equally mental or "subjective" and real. "I must be dreadfully worried today, Bruno Bluthgeld said to himself. For now an even graver alteration in his sense-perception was setting in, and one unfamiliar to him. A dull, smoky cast was beginning to settle over all the environment around him, making the buildings and cars seem like inert, gloomy mounds, without color or motion" (*Dr. Bloodmoney*, 280). The description blends the subjective disturbance with the objective catastrophe. It leaves us in a sort of state of indecision: is it me or the world that has lost its equilibrium? And the response never varies: both.

Generally speaking, individuals—and the Earth itself—undergo a destruction or a death that makes Dick's characters survivors. If historical time is the time of human life, prehistoric or posthistoric life is the time of survivors. Here, we rediscover one of SF's recurring characters, whose prototype is a sort of Robinson figure. It isn't by mere chance that Jules Verne, a pioneer of SF, wrote multiple robinsonades.[5] SF often gives us characters who are confronted by an unknown world in which they need to survive while at the same time attempting to figure out its laws. Even when they have sophisticated tools at their disposal, they are condemned to live forever by their wits, because nothing ever turns out as it was supposed to. In his American form, Robinson is an everyman, an ordinary adventurer, a frontiersman, a self-made man, a colonizer, and a bricoleur.

This is particularly true in Dick's work. His characters are ordinary individuals doing everything they can to stay afloat. Like all SF authors, he devises interstellar battles and intergalactic conflicts, but that doesn't prevent him from always basing his plots on an ordinary person wrestling with personal, financial, marital, and professional problems that have nothing whatsoever to do with the destiny of humanity. His protagonists never occupy an elevated position in the social hierarchy.[6] They are record dealers, repairmen, potters, artisans, and employees; they have lowly occupations, like the famous "tire regroover" of *Our Friends from Frolix 8*. On a desert planet or on a planet devastated by war, there's no other choice but to be a bricoleur, to patch together whatever you find scattered amidst the debris. The bricoleur is the ordinary hero in Dick, the figure that is diametrically opposed to the engineer or the android human-machine. "The handies are the most valuable people in the world."[7]

The Dickian bricoleur corresponds perfectly to the definition given by Lévi-Strauss, when he distinguishes the bricoleur from the engineer. Unlike the latter, what characterizes the bricoleur is that he has no preexisting project to which he subordinates the series of his tasks: "His universe of instruments is closed, and the rule of his game is always to make do with 'whatever is at hand'—that is to say, a set of tools and materials that is finite at each moment, as well as heterogeneous [. . .]."[8] He accumulates the most varied kinds of objects, things that are totally out of the ordinary, yet the reason for this accumulation doesn't obey any predefined project; instead, it is based upon the instrumentality of the stock with which the bricoleur is "in a kind of dialogue" (the famous "this could always come in handy"). He constantly asks himself what the elements making up his stock might "mean," what they could be used for, but this interaction takes place within a restricted set of possibilities, insofar as each element, having been used before, retains the predetermined character of its previous usages.

This restricted scope is what, for Lévi-Strauss, constitutes the bricoleur's essential difference from the engineer. The engineer uses concepts to seek ways to go beyond the constraints imposed by the state of knowledge at a given moment, while the bricoleur always remains within those constraints because of the restrictions imposed by his stock. What he puts together can only be made with what is on hand, even if, within these limits, he develops invaluable, intuitive relations that reveal affinities and relations of sympathy with the elements of his stock—outside of all conceptuality.[9] It is precisely not on the basis of concepts that his work proceeds, but on the basis of the signs that his stock suggests to him.

Translated into Dickian terms, bricolage is an activity that relates to the right hemisphere, to the hemisphere of *gestalts*, of dynamisms or schemata capable of perceiving the potentialities of a nonverbal reality. It shouldn't surprise us that we encounter so many bricoleurs, artisans, and repairmen in his novels. But they are there, first and foremost, to be opposed to the engineers, the technicians, the industrialists, and all forms of technocracy. If the engineer tends toward the dehumanized android, it is because of the primacy she accords to the abstractions of concepts, symbols, and their algorithms. Everything takes place as if the acquisition of technological expertise had separated humanity from artisanal know-how, from the plasticity of intuitions, and from schemata developed through contact with matter. Dick deplores the fact that technical machines lead to such specialization and to a hy-pertelic form of the brain.

The novella "The Variable Man" is probably the most definitive stag-ing of this opposition. A war is brewing between the Earth and alien invaders, but the Terrans don't want to commit themselves while the probabilities calculated by their computers still don't fall in their favor. In the meantime, the Terran generals are looking for a weapon that will give them a decisive advantage. The situation grows more complicated when a spatio-temporal bubble returns from the past with a repairman from the twentieth century. His arrival interferes with the computer cal-culations such that they no longer predict there being any possibility of victory. The bricoleur is "something from which no inference can be made" (S1, 210), because his talents are a challenge to the specialized knowledge and cerebral programming of the engineers and techni-cians. "We're specialized. Each of us has his own line, his own work. I understand my work, you understand yours. [. . .] This man is different. He can fix anything, do anything. He doesn't work with knowledge, with science—the classified accumulation of facts. He *knows* nothing. It's not in his head, a form of learning. He works by intuition—his power is in his hands, not his head" (S1, 227).[10]

What makes the bricoleur so interesting isn't just that she reacti-vates the intuitive power of the right hemisphere, but also that she is able to *reroute* the predetermined elements of her stock, making them serve a purpose that is altogether different than the one that they were initially intended for. With bricolage, the imagination becomes a faculty that allows us to deviate from existing ends, a process of diversion or deformation. We could certainly compare bricolage with *art brut* or *art naïf*, as Lévi-Strauss proposes, but we could also compare it with Dada or with the "neo-dada" works of Jasper Johns and Robert Rauschenberg, in which they recycle heterogeneous materials by diverting them from their intended uses.

In his discussion of Robert Rauschenberg's works, Leo Steinberg reproaches formalist critics for treating "modern painting as an evolving technology wherein at any one moment specific tasks require solution—tasks set for the artist as problems are set for researchers in the big corporations. The artist as engineer and research technician becomes important insofar as he comes up with solutions to the right problem."[11] According to the formalist, the artist is described as a highly specialized engineer. Conversely, if Steinberg invokes the works of Rauschenberg and Jasper Johns, it is in order to propose a figure of the artist that is much closer to the bricoleur, because, like her, they make use of heterogeneous elements—tissues, newspaper clippings, socks, fans, and so on—which they divert from their initial uses. We know that Rauschenberg called one of his series of works "Combines," which is a fitting term for such assemblages. It is a matter of starting from "any receptor surface on which objects are scattered, on which data is entered, on which any information may be received, printed, impressed—whether coherently or in confusion."[12] The technological model falls apart because of the heterogeneous and well-worn character of the elements composing these works of bricolage. Only machines like those of Tinguely remain or, as Steinberg says, disparate accumulations that are like maps of a brain saturated with information.[13]

Recuperation and diversion are two essential aspects of bricolage, as they are of (neo)dadaism. The bricoleur hijacks items that are intended for an established end or ensemble and recuperates them with an eye to other functions and uses. Of the two figures between which she finds herself, the engineer and the artist, she is closest to the artist, even if her powers of invention are limited by the predetermined aims of her stock. Yet, in Dick's eyes, this limitation is less constraining than the limitations imposed on the brain by linguistic, digital codes, as we can see in his portrait of the "variable man," whom he describes in terms quite close to Korzybski's: "An intuition more in his hands than in his head. A kind of genius, such as a painter or a pianist has. [. . .] He has no verbal knowledge about things, no semantic references. He deals with the things themselves. Directly" (S1, 263).[14]

The power of diversion doesn't just distance the bricoleur from the engineer and bring her into proximity with the artist; it also brings her close to the counterfeiter or the hacker, inasmuch as this power relates to various forms of deprogramming and piracy. "The ethics most important for the survival of the true, human individual would be: Cheat, lie, evade, fake it, be elsewhere, forge documents, build improved electronic gadgets in your garage that'll outwit the gadgets used by the authorities."[15] From this point of view, the bricoleur fights against the generalized androidization of the social realm. She preserves a form of inventiveness and vitality that resists being enclosed in a world where all decisions have already been made for you and where the purpose of every object, especially those that have become "intelligent," predetermines the uses to which they can be put—unless, of course, they're being used to scramble the software. "—'We've been making statistical reports on society for two centuries. We have immense files of data.

The machines are able to predict what each person and group will do at a given time, in a given situation. But this man is beyond all prediction. He's a variable. It's contrary to science.'—'The indeterminate particle.'—'What's that?'—'The particle that moves in such a way that we can't predict what position it will occupy at a given second. Random. The random particle."[16]

For Dick, this isn't a matter of reactivating the heroic figure of Robinson the colonizer. The bricoleur's aim is not to appropriate a world by establishing the conditions for its expansion, but to assemble fragments of heterogeneous worlds so that she can circulate between them. The Dickian hero is always a modest individual, but one whose unpredictable character of being a "random particle" makes him superior to the grand figures of political and social domination. "I know only one thing about my novels. In them, again and again, this minor man asserts himself in all his hasty, sweaty strength. [. . .] Everything is on a small scale. Collapse is enormous; the positive little figure outlined against the universal rubble is [. . .] gnat-sized in scope, finite in what he can do . . . and yet in some sense great."[17] In the face of personal problems that are shaking up "his" world, he immediately finds himself confronted by other worlds, vaster worlds that are better organized and more impressive than "his own," but whose organization he will shake up in turn as he simply goes about the business of solving his problems.

As Dick emphasizes, the opposition between the bricoleur and the engineer doesn't just concern the differing natures of their activities, but also measures their degree of social integration, as if the extent of their technical competence were directly proportional to their compliance with the social order. Given his restricted stock of materials and tools, the bricoleur's range of action is limited. He clearly can't work for a major corporation, or if so, only at a subordinate level, which is why the bricoleur often finds himself on the margins of society, sometimes even at the limits of social "misadjustment." The engineer, on the contrary, is always engaged in a vast technological network. His highly specialized work integrates him into a sort of megamachine born of the functional synergy between different technical systems. But he only becomes an effective cog on the condition that he complies with the social order and preexisting techniques that are imposed on him by the megamachine as it grows larger and larger, ceaselessly absorbing technical skills, social adaptations, and politico-economical strategies into itself.

The environment in which the bricoleur lives is much less organized and doesn't demand the same sort of adaptation. One gets the impression that, because of her relative "marginality," she needs to reconstruct her social order over and over again. Her bricolage isn't limited to tinkering with gadgets in her little corner of the world; she attempts to repair an unhinged social order and to adjust it toward other ends. She lives in a world where the social order is at the very least precarious, if it hasn't already fallen to pieces, torn apart by conflicts and wars, by the implosions of psyches—to such an extent that she can hardly even tell what world she's in anymore. You can no longer tell who is human and who has ceased to be; you can no longer tell who is living and who is dead; you can no longer tell who is real and who is artificial. Every time, everything needs to be reconstructed. Perhaps this, then, is the Dickian *caritas*: to become the repairman of a machine-world that has been unhinged by armies of engineers, who, for their part, have been persuaded to try and get the greatest yield possible from it.

It is in this sense that the bricoleur is the figure of the time after. She comes after the destruction. What do you do in a world that has been half destroyed by atomic explosions and psychic implosions? You have no other choice than to gather the pieces together, to patch them up and begin mending the fragments of the world—though not with the aim of reconstructing the world of before, of rebuilding that unlivable and destructive world, but in order to create truly new pockets of livable worlds, to create a form of living continuity by promoting the circulation of sympathies. *Repairing is not the same thing as restoring* and is even its opposite. Maybe humanity doesn't know it in the beginning, but humans are creating unlivable worlds and perfect though irrevocable machines, all of which are making the bricoleur the figure of the future.

Dick believes in the social force of these modest individuals and in the reparative power of their bricolage. The point isn't to think with grand totalities beyond the scope of all individual action (Society, Capitalism, "the" World), but to show how those totalities collapse. If Dick makes them collapse, it is so he can reconstruct them and patch them back together differently. We are going to reconstruct a world, but in our own way, with whatever we have on hand. That is the way alliances, communities, and bands of repairmen come together in Dick's works. His novels always describe segments of a world that could be made better because an individual or a group of individuals find themselves confronted by a problem that requires them to cobble together solutions as bricoleurs. The reality of the world is not given, it needs to be constructed and what it will become depends upon the active part played by every individual, upon the actions they undertake with one another, here and now.

In Dick, we never live in either the worst or the best of all possible worlds, but in a world that could be improved or repaired. From this point of view, he shares the conviction of William James, who declares himself to be

> against bigness and greatness in all their forms, and with the invisible
> molecular moral forces that work from individual to individual, stealing
> in through the crannies of the world like so many soft rootlets, or like
> the capillary oozing of water, and yet rending the hardest monuments
> of man's pride, if you give them time. The bigger the unit you deal with,
> the hollower, the more brutal, the more mendacious is the life dis-
> played. So I am against all big organizations as such, national ones
> first and foremost; against all big successes and big results; and in
> favor of the eternal forces of truth which always work in the individual
> and immediately unsuccessful way, under-dogs always, till history
> comes, after they are long dead, and puts them on the top.[18]

The opposition between the bricoleur and the engineer in Dick is another form of the opposition between these interindividual alliances, which act gradually, and the grand totalities that act through "global-ization." That is why Dick's characters are often on the verge of deso-cialization and vaguely "misadjusted." On the margins where they live, they are free to resocialize otherwise than in a manner according to the expectations of a world that excludes them.

This force that individuals have is inseparable, in Dick, from a form of *irresponsibility*, either because the social responsibilities are too great to bear or because their social status exempts them. In the same way that high positions are said to come with high responsibility, we should speak of Dick's characters as being *minimally responsible*—or highly irresponsible. If they succeed in solving problems that are beyond them, it isn't because of their sense of responsibility but rather because of their fundamental irresponsibility. Their continuous bricolage contains a portion of play that keeps them in the state of being a "social minority," as Simondon says, linking that state to a form of childhood. The bricoleur is a sort of child at play, who unintentionally unhinges the "real" world of the highly responsible people. This echoes the admiration Dick has for the intrinsic power of youth as a spontaneously disobedient, irresponsible force. There is a profound optimism in Dick in this respect. Youth's strength lies in its irresponsibility, especially if responsibility consists in making oneself complicit with the coercions imposed in the name of a "reality" that is raised to the level of a principle the moment it comes time to turn to "serious things." It is plain to see: Dick's characters lack seriousness.

Dick rightly distinguishes between two cases of disobedience: those who disobey for reasons of political or theoretical militantism and those who disobey quite simply because of "a mere lack of agreement that one must always do what one is ordered to do—especially when the order comes from a posted, printed sign. In both cases there is disobedience. We might applaud the first as meaningful. The second, merely irresponsible. And yet it is in the second that I see a happier future."[19] This is clearly due to the indeterminate part of that irresponsible, rebel matter: namely, the lack of seriousness that, for Dick, is constitutive of youth. The point isn't that Dick valorizes the absence of political con-

sciousness but that he prefers a form of vitality that strives to piece together a new reality through bricolage, rather than giving in to the imperatives of the "dominant" reality. Once again, repairing and mending
everything that the artificial worlds destroy, abandon, and exclude. "I
have never had too high a regard for what is generally called 'reality.'
Reality, to me, is not so much something that you perceive, but something you make. *You create it more rapidly than it creates you.*"[20]

But there is still another reason why Dick privileges the figure of the
bricoleur. Lévi-Strauss connects bricolage with mythical thought, understood as a sort of "intellectual bricolage," just as bricolage itself
has a "mythopoetic" character.[21] This is because mythology, too, operates on the basis of an extensive, yet limited, heterogeneous reper-
toire of mythemes. But doesn't SF find itself in the same situation at
the moment when Dick begins to write: a finite ensemble of stereotypical and arbitrary conventions with which authors must ceaselessly
(re)compose their stories? Aliens, mad scientists, intrepid adventurers,
spaceships, ultramodern technology, inexplicable phenomena, etc.—
a whole ensemble of indefinitely recomposable mythemes. Only, in its
case, the one thing standing in the way of bricolage is the industrial-
ization of the genre, its serialization through the production of magazines (pulps), which requires such a rate of productivity from authors
that they are forced to reuse the same recipes over and over again. Inventiveness remains circumscribed within preestablished scenarios.[22]

Among a few others, Dick was one of the authors who quickly freed
themselves from these imposed figures. It is as if he had derailed—
and derided—all of the "mythemes" of the genre: linear causality, unity

of worlds, fearlessness of the adventurer, hostile aliens, not to mention all the scattered elements that he injects into his novels in the manner of a Rauschenberg composition. We can cite at random: Jungian psychoanalysis, the *Tibetan Book of the Dead*, psychiatric and medical literature, biblical texts, esoteric texts, information theory, the writings of Korzybski, Burroughs, Jung, Binswanger . . . and not only as sources of inspiration but as materials to be recuperated and used by means of assemblage in his constructions.[23]

In the end, isn't the bricoleur, isn't the "random particle," Dick himself? Isn't he the one who makes worlds fall to pieces, the one who takes the categories imposed on stories and smashes them to bits? Isn't the portrait of the "variable man" actually a self-portrait, that of an artisan who cobbles together his stories like a bricoleur in his little corner of the world?

> What I write doesn't make a whole lot of sense. There is fun & religion & psychotic horror strewn about like a bunch of hats. Also, there is a social or sociological drift—rather than toward the hard sciences. [. . .] Everything is equally real, like junk jewels in the alley. [. . .] I certainly see the randomness in my work, & I also see how this fast shuffling of possibility after possibility might eventually, given enough time, juxtapose & disclose something important & automatically overlooked in more orderly thinking.[24]

If novels can break away from a linear plot and bifurcate ceaselessly following unpredictable developments, this is because they are constructed upon the metastable zone of the "fantastic," where worlds interfere with one another, where the categories—causality, identity, reality—collapse, getting as close to chaos as possible. "Every novel of mine is at least two novels superimposed. This is the origin; this is why they are full of loose ends, but also, it is impossible to predict the outcome, since there is no linear plot as such."[25] Yet, there really is a reparative dimension in his novels, in the sense that we need to repair the worlds, we need to patch up our psychic integrity, in whatever way we can, even if it means filling in the gaps with deliria. The artist's three tasks are something like the following: *recuperate* the materials abandoned by the artificial worlds, *divert* them from their predefined uses, and *repair* the physical and mental worlds that the forces of regression and entropy destroy.

Even if Dick confesses to having a secret "love of chaos," chaos is also what the writing of novels should protect him from, much like the schizophrenic bricoleurs, who bring together heterogeneous elements in their constructions in an attempt to gather themselves back together.[26] It is necessary to bring incompatible elements together in the novel, to find the form that will allow them to be gathered together, in order to ward off the danger of their dispersal. Maybe that is ultimately the most important aspect of bricolage: protecting oneself from the dangers of madness. Bricolage is another name for delirium. Isn't delirium a sort of reparative, schizophrenic bricolage?

Everything takes place as if Dick had never had *any ground*, any ultimate certitude to hold onto. "Every idea thought of is true *but for no measurable length of time* because it—i.e., its truth—is instantly negated by an *equal and opposite idea*, and so forth [. . .]. Each self passes through an infinitude of universes or 'frames,' each with laws—truths—of its own."[27] This is particularly apparent in *The Exegesis*, which multiplies hypotheses and theories, sending them every which way. "Theories are like planes at LA International: a new one along every minute."[28] He even has a hypothesis to explain this incessant proliferation of contradictory hypotheses: his brain needs to create a scramble of conflicting ideas, "like white *noise*," like an indecipherable code meant to protect him from a revelation that is too important (*Exegesis*, 494). The multiplication of hypotheses and stories would then be an act of panicked and incessant foreclosure. His mind would be in a constant state of vertigo, only ever able to slide or drift from one idea to the next, except for when the bricolage of his novels allows him temporarily to settle it.

INTRODUCTION

1. [Throughout this book, Lapoujade refers to "SF" without ever spelling out either *la science-fiction* or *la fiction spéculative*. While Dick is often thought of as a classic "sci-fi" author, his work, as Lapoujade shows, often challenges and exceeds any traditional conception of the genre. I have chosen to retain "SF" throughout to leave open the possibility of reading it either as science fiction or, more generally, as speculative fiction.—TN]

2. Kingsley Amis, *New Maps of Hell*, 126 ff.

3. It is generally thought that the term "science-fiction," in the sense in which we understand it today, began to spread in the 1930s, at the time when pulp novels were first beginning to appear.

4. Aristotle, *Topics*, A, 5, 101a–102b.

5. More recently, one could look to the logicist philosophical theories regarding possible worlds, from Saul Kripke up to the modal realism of David Lewis, which borrow many examples from science fiction. On the history of the notion of "possible worlds," see Jacob Schmutz's article, "Qui a inventé les mondes possibles?" For a literary exploration of the theory of these possible worlds, see Françoise Lavocat, ed., *La Théorie littéraire des mondes possibles*.

6. Philip K. Dick, "How to Build a Universe That Doesn't Fall Apart Two Days Later," 262. [Throughout this book, Lapoujade quotes from four essays by Dick, all of which are collected in *The Shifting Realities of Philip K. Dick*, edited

by Lawrence Sutin: "How to Build a Universe That Doesn't Fall Apart Two Days Later," "If You Find This World Bad, You Should See Some of the Others," "Introduction to *The Golden Man*," and "The Android and the Human." Citations refer to the page numbers from that volume.—TN]

7. "Adjustment Team," S2, 332. [All references to Dick's stories cite the five-volume *Complete Stories*, published by Subterranean Press between 2010 and 2014. The volumes are cited in the notes as S1–S5, respectively.—TN]

8. [In the introduction to his *Philosophy through the Looking Glass*, Jean-Jacques Lecercle offers four arguments in favor of the *untranslatability* of the French term *délire* and subsequently leaves it (and its related forms, *délirer* and *délirant*) untranslated throughout the book. Despite the validity of Lecercle's arguments and their applicability to the present study (we might say that Lapoujade's "versions of Philip K. Dick" situate him within the "suppressed tradition of *délire*"), I have opted to use "delirium" (and its related forms) throughout this book for the sake of its readability. I hope that in consistently using the English cognate, even where an alternative term (such as "delusion") might have fit more seamlessly, I have retained sufficient reference to the significance of this concept. For readers interested in a fuller discussion of this issue, see. *Philosophy through the Looking Glass*, 1–14.—TN]

9. "How to Build a Universe," 262: "So I ask, in my writing, What is real? Because unceasingly we are bombarded with pseudorealities manufactured by very sophisticated people using very sophisticated electronic mechanisms. I do not distrust their motives; I distrust their power. They have a lot of it. And it is an astonishing power: that of creating whole universes, universes of the mind. I ought to know. I do the same thing."

10. Philip K. Dick, "Introduction to *The Golden Man*," 92. [Lapoujade cites the introduction to *Gradhiva*, no. 29 by Pierre Déléage and Emmanuel Grimaud, "Anomalie. Champ faible, niveau légumes," which quotes these lines (12).—TN]

11. "The Day Mr. Computer Fell Out of Its Tree," S5, 380.

12. "Holy Quarrel," S5, 187–88. In "The Day Mr. Computer Fell Out of Its Tree," a computer experiences psychotic episodes, because it "had absorbed too much freaked-out input" (S5, 380).

13. Sass, *The Paradoxes of Delusion*, 21.

14. Foucault, *Psychiatric Power*, 132: "The psychiatrist, as he will function in the space of asylum discipline, will no longer be the individual who considers what the mad person says from the standpoint of truth, but will switch resolutely, definitively, to the standpoint of reality [. . .]. The psychiatrist is someone who [. . .] must ensure that reality has the supplement of power necessary for it to impose itself on madness and, conversely, he is someone who must remove from madness its power to avoid reality."

15. Foucault, 132 [This phrase would be found on page 166, but the sentence has been omitted from the English translation. My translation.—TN]

16. Foucault, 135.

17. See Dick's letter to Ursula K. Le Guin, reproduced in *The Exegesis* (48): "The spirit when he arrived here looked around, saw Richard Nixon and those creatures, and was so wrath-filled that he never stopped writing letters to Washington until Nixon was out. [. . .] You wouldn't believe his animosity toward the tyrannies both here and in the USSR; he saw them as twin horns of the same evil entity—one vast worldwide state whose basic nature was clear to him as being one of slavery, a continuation of Rome itself."

18. This is Terry Carr, editor of the "Ace Double" collection, which would publish two SF novels in a single volume, tête-bêche. See Sutin, 66.

19. Philip K. Dick, "If You Find This World Bad, You Should See Some of the Others," 234.

1. WORLDS

1. Foucault, *The Order of Things*, 47. See also Alfred Schütz's 1946 article, "Don Quixote and the Problem of Reality."

2. "Although originally I presumed that the differences between these worlds was caused entirely by the subjectivity of the various human viewpoints, it did not take me long to open the question as to whether it might not be more than that—that in fact plural realities did exist superimposed onto one another like so many film transparencies" (If You Find This World Bad . . . ," 240).

3. Spinrad, "The Transmogrification of Philip K. Dick," 209. [Lapoujade cites the French translation in the volume edited by Hélène Collon, *Regards sur Philip K. Dick.*—TN]

4. "Philip K. Dick in Interview with D. Scott Apel and Kevin C. Briggs," 47: ". . . I have this feeling we live in a pluraverse rather than a universe. . . . " [Lapoujade cites the French translation of this interview in *Regards sur Philip K. Dick.*—TN]

5. See the description of KR-3, the drug in *Flow My Tears, the Policeman Said*, which forces "anyone affected by it . . . to perceive irreal universes, whether they want to or not. As I said, trillions of possibilities are theoretically all of a sudden real; chance enters and the person's percept system chooses one possibility out of all those presented to it. It *has* to choose, because if it didn't, competing universes would overlap, and the concept of space itself would vanish" (841).

6. *Eye in the Sky* first appeared in French under the title *Les Mondes divergents* [*The Divergent Worlds*].

7. Kim Stanley Robinson, *The Novels of Philip K. Dick*, 16: "Hamilton has lost his job working for the defense industry because he was once slightly involved with socialists. His friend has lost his job because he is black. The *koinos kosmos* is now seen to be composed of individual visions similar to those that Hamilton has just suffered; it is equal parts religious fanaticism, moralistic prudery, fearful paranoia, and political extremism."

8. Sutin, 80–81.

2. CAUSALITY

1. On this point, we will refer the reader to Quentin Meillassoux's essential observations in *Science Fiction and Extro-Science Fiction*.

2. Dick discovered the *I Ching* (or Book of Transformations) through his longstanding interest in Jung. It was in 1949 that Jung wrote the foreword to the English translation of the *I Ching*, which he connected to his theory of synchronicity (each of the hexagrammes being an expression of unconscious archetypes). On this point, see Sutin, 109–10. [See Jung's foreword in the Bollingen edition of the *I Ching*, xxi ff.—TN]

3. On the relation between causality and synchronicity in Dick, see the important article by Katherine Hayles, "Metaphysics and Metafiction in *The Man in the High Castle*."

4. *The Man in the High Castle*, 62. The idea of "living books" returns often in Dick's works. There are even books whose text is rewritten as reality changes (see *Nick and the Glimmung* and the story "Not by Its Cover, S5).

5. The story "The Commuter" explores a similar theme, namely, that of a possible reality that is so close to being realized (the project of constructing a city, rejected by a single vote) that it acquires a form of existence, at least for one character—who is himself evanescent—and who is trying to get to this nearly real city where he lives. "Maybe certain parts of the past were unstable" (S2, 167), allowing the possible reality to exist in an interval. The story's protagonist manages to visit the nonexistent city but fears that his own world would become unreal if he were to stay too long.

6. See also what he says later of the Torah: "Everything is written down and has been written down from the beginning, as the Jews knew from the disclosure of the Torah. Basically, sacred history exists as information[. . .]. *The mythic ritual is an entry key into the sacred narrative.* It functions the way an entry key of a computer functions vis-à-vis a given program" (*Exegesis*, 606).

7. See Norbert Wiener, *The Human Use of Human Beings*, 50–51, where the struggle between information and disorder refers to a theological struggle that the scientist wages against two types of divinity (the Manichaean and Augustinian devils).

3. THE THINKING THING

1. "Retreat Syndrome," S5, 103.

2. *Our Friends from Frolix 8*, 81–82: "—'Did Jung stress the point that one of these archetypes could, at any time, absorb you? And a reformation of your self would never reoccur? You would be only a talking walking extension of the archetype?'—'Of course he stressed it. But it's not at night in sleep that the archetype takes over, it's during the day. When they appear during the day—that's when you're destroyed.'"

3. "I Hope I Shall Arrive Soon," S5, 441–42.

4. *Martian Time-Slip*, 64. See also the psychiatrist's response to a billionaire who controls Mars and demands much of his entourage: "It's people like you with your harsh driving demands that create schizophrenics" (169).

5. "The Chromium Fence," S3, 354. Of the comic stories dealing with psychoanalysis, we can mention "Recall Mechanism" (S4), in which a character who is a "precog" consults a psychoanalyst, not because of an old repressed trauma, but because of a traumatic episode that has yet to occur. He has received phobic warnings from the future since he was a kid, and now, the more sessions he has, the greater his anxiety grows.

6. Here, we must pay tribute to John E. Mack, the very serious professor of psychiatry at the Harvard Medical School, who was persuaded, on the basis of multiple testimonies, that some of his patients had been victims of alien abductions. See his book *Abduction*, as well as Jean-Claude Maleval's *Logique du délire*, which cites it (17).

7. See Watzlawick, *The Language of Change*, 21ff.

8. This work was adapted as a film by Richard Linklater in 2006.

9. *A Scanner Darkly*, 948–49. The book's title is an allusion to the phrase from Saint Paul, cited by the Japanese dignitary in *The Man in the High Castle* after he was plunged into an alternate world.

10. *A Scanner Darkly*, 1005. See also the effects of the drug in *Flow My Tears, the Policeman Said*: "A drug such as KR-3 breaks down the brain's ability to exclude one unit of space out of another. [. . .] When this occurs the brain can no longer exclude alternative spatial vectors. It opens up the entire range of spatial variation. The brain can no longer tell which objects exist and which are only latent, unspatial possibilities" (840–41).

11. Compare Freud, *The Schreber Case*, 60: "What we take to be the production of the illness, the formation of the delusion, is in reality the attempt at a cure, the reconstruction." Dick rediscovers the reparative function of delirium in his own way, through the multiplication of delirious hypotheses in the *Exegesis*. "But I sense something more: what I think of as a *reweaving* of me" (*Exegesis*, 220). See also *Exegesis*, 515.

12. *Exegesis*, 341. And also, 22: "I seem to be living in my own novels more and more. I can't figure out why. Am I losing touch with reality? Or is reality actually sliding toward a Phil Dickian type of atmosphere?"

13. Three novels that Dick wrote in the years following the religious experience of March 1974 were published under this title: *VALIS* (1978), *The Divine Invasion* (1980), and *The Transmigration of Timothy Archer* (1982). A prologue to the series, *Radio Free Albemuth*, was written in 1976 but published only after Dick's death.

14. *Radio Free Albemuth*, 180: "—'This 'telepathic sender who overpowered you with his personality' is in your own head. Broadcasting from the other side of your skull. From previously unused brain tissue.'—'I thought you favored the alternate universe theory,' I said, surprised.—'[. . .] Instead of another parallel universe, more likely it's a parallel hemisphere in your head.'"

15. *VALIS*, 327–28: "—'The information was fired at my friend Horselover Fat.'—'But that's you. "Philip" means "Horselover" in Greek, lover of horses.

"Fat" is the German translation of "Dick." So you've translated your name.'—I said nothing."

16. See, for example, 178: "The night before, Bob and I—I mean, Bob and Horselover Fat [. . .]"; or 203: "In all my reading I have—I mean, Horselover Fat has—never found anything [. . .]."

17. *VALIS*, 348: "Horselover Fat was gone forever. As if he had never existed.—'I don't understand,' I said. 'You destroyed him.'—'Yes,' the child said.—I said, 'Why?'—'To make you whole.'—'Then he's in me? Alive in me?'—'Yes.'"

18. *The Game-Players of Titan*, 144–45: "Each perception and observation which Dave Mutreaux had rejected in himself existed here, imperishable, living on in a kind of half-life, feeding deeply on his psychic energy. He could not be held responsible for these, and yet there they were anyhow, semi-autonomous and—feral. Opposed to everything Mutreaux consciously, deliberately believed in. In opposition to all his life aims."

19. See Étienne Balibar, *Identity and Difference*.

20. See the remark in "If You Find This World Bad . . . ," 248: "if an entire country can overnight forget *one* thing they all know, they can forget *other things*, more important things; in fact, overwhelmingly important things. I am writing about amnesia on the part of millions of people, of, so to speak, fake memories laid down. This theme of faked memories is a constant thread in my writing over the years."

21. See also the short story, "The Electric Ant" (S5, 275ff), which tells the story of a man who discovers through a surgical operation that he is really an android. This is the same uncertainty that is expressed by the bounty hunter in *Do Androids Dream of Electric Sheep?*, who is asked if he isn't himself an android, similar to those he is supposed to eliminate.

22. Philip K. Dick, "The Android and the Human," 201: "In the field of abnormal psychology, the schizoid personality structure is well defined; in it there is a continual paucity of feeling [. . .]. Anyhow, there is a certain parallel between what I call the "android" personality and the schizoid."

4. ON THE FANTASTIC

1. See Heraclitus (Kahn), 31: "The world of the waking is one and shared, but the sleeping turn aside each into his private world." Dick often returns to this distinction. See, for instance, *The Exegesis*, 65; *The Zap Gun*, 24–25; and his remarks on *Eye in the Sky* in Sutin, 92: "It's like 'Eye' when actual rescue is right at hand but they can't wake up. Yes, we are asleep like they are in 'Eye' & we must wake up & see past (through) the dream—the spurious world with its own time—to the rescue *outside*—outside *now*, not later."

2. Todorov, *The Fantastic*, 25.

3. Freud, *The Psychopathology of Everyday Life*, 311–24.

4. On fright, see Jean Laplanche's analyses in *Problématiques I*, 55ff. [See also the entry on "Fright" in Jean Laplanche and Jean-Bertrand Pontalis, *The Language of Psycho-Analysis*, 174–75.—TN]

5. *The Three Stigmata of Palmer Eldritch*, 312.

6. Merleau-Ponty, *The Visible and the Invisible*, 5: "[. . .] the intrinsic, descriptive differences between the dream and the perceived take on ontological value. And we answer Pyrrhonism sufficiently by showing that there is a difference of structure and, as it were, of grain between the perception or true vision [. . .] and the dream [. . .]."

7. On this point, see Quentin Meillassoux's analyses in *Science Fiction and Extro-Science Fiction*, especially his analysis of the Kantian transcendental deduction and its confrontation with the "oneiric scene" of cinnabar, 28–31.

8. Sartre, *The Imaginary*, 159ff. Despite his reservations about psychoanalysis, he agrees with Freud on this point: the dream is isolated, reduced to a psychic scenery. On this closure of the dream in Freud, see André Green, "De l''Esquisse' à 'L'interprétation des rêves': coupure et clôture," 173, 177.

9. See Freud's "Formulations Regarding the Two Principles in Mental Functioning," 3–4: "In place of repression . . . there developed an impartial *passing*

of judgement, which had to decide whether a particular idea was true or false, that is, was in agreement with reality or not."

10. Husserl, *Experience and Judgment*, 30. Compare Merleau-Ponty, *The Visible and the Invisible*, 3ff.

11. See Dadoun, "Les ombilics du rêve," 241. [The phrase "a mosaic of blasts" (*une mosaïque d'éclats*), the sentence before, is quoted from Dadoun's essay, which in turn is quoting Artaud's *L'Ombilic des limbes,* to which the essay's title also refers. See Victor Corti's translation, "Umbilical Limbo," in *Collected Works of Antonin Artaud*, vol. 1, 50.—TN]

12. Foucault, "Dream, Imagination, and Existence," 59.

13. Henri Bergson, "Dreams," 125.

14. Compare Freud's famous remark in *The Interpretation of Dreams*, 507: "[The dream-work] does not think, calculate or judge in any way at all; it restricts itself to giving things a new form."

15. See, for example, the drug that makes you lose your power of judgment in the story "Misadjustment," S3, 372: "*The P-K makes his delusion work. Therefore in a sense it isn't a delusion . . . not unless you can stand far enough back, get a long way off and compare his warped area with the world proper. But how can the P-K himself do that? He has no objective standard; he can't very well get away from himself, and the warp follows him wherever he goes.*"

16. Antonin Artaud, "Witchcraft and Cinema," 66 [translation modified]. See also his note to the screenplay of *La Coquille et le Clergyman*, 20: "This scenario is not the reproduction of a dream and must not be regarded as such. I shall not try to excuse its apparent inconsistency by the facile subterfuge of dreams. Dreams have more than their logic. They have their life where nothing but an intelligent and somber truth appears" [translation modified].

17. Maybe Lynch had to confront both oneirism (in *Mulholland Drive*) and SF (in *Dune*) to renounce two possible orientations of his fantastic. On the status of dreams, clichés, the fantastic in Lynch, see Pierre Alferi, *Des enfants et des monstres*, 221ff.

18. On the disappearance of perceptive faith or transcendental confidence, see Ludwig Binswanger, *Melancholie und Manie*, 15ff. [or the French translation (cited in the original), 22ff.—TN]. And on the influence of Binswanger and psychiatric literature on Dick, see Anthony Wolk, "The Swiss Connection," 114–15.

19. "Fantasy involves that which general opinion regards as impossible, science fiction involves that which general opinion regards as possible under the right circumstances. This is in essence a judgment-call," quoted in Sutin, 75.

20. "Exhibit Piece," S3, 196.

21. See Gilbert Simondon, *Individuation in Light of Notions of Form and Information*, vol. 1, 233: "The *fluctuatio animi* that precedes the resolute action is not a hesitation between several objects or even several paths, but an unstable collection of incompatible, almost similar, and therefore disparate, ensembles. The subject before action is caught between several worlds. . . . "

22. *VALIS*, 335: "This is the danger of the archetypes; the opposite qualities are not yet separated. Bipolarization into paired opposites does not occur until consciousness occurs." See also *Flow My Tears, the Policeman Said*, 716: "It seemed to him as if he sat behind the tiller of his custom-made unique quibble, facing a red light, green light, amber light all at once; no rational response was possible. [. . .] The terrible power, he thought, of illogic. Of the archetypes. Operating out of the drear depths of the collective unconscious which joined him and her—and everyone else—together."

5. ENTROPY AND REGRESSION

1. See also the novel *Counter-Clock World*, in which time runs in reverse, the dead return to life, exhumations replace interments, vitariums replace funerariums, adults return "back to childhood and finally to babyhood and then back into a womb" (58), etc.

2. Ludwig Binswanger, *The Case of Ellen West*, 305ff. The "tomb world"

appears frequently in Dick's work, notably in *Do Androids Dream of Electric Sheep?* Foucault, in his introduction to Binswanger's *Dream and Existence*, emphasizes the impossibility of all becoming for Ellen West: "For Ellen West, the solid space of real movement, the space where things come to be, has progressively, bit by bit, disappeared" (63).

3. Dick rediscovers this regression in the depths of the ocean. "The underwater world [. . .] is a place of dead things, a place where everything rots and falls into despair and ruin. [. . .] It's a world made up of its own self, entirely separate from ours. With its own wretched laws, under which everything must decline into rubbish. A world dominated by the force of unyielding entropy and nothing else," *Galactic Pot-Healer*, 102–3.

4. Lem, "Philip K. Dick: A Visionary among the Charlatans," 125–26, as well as the profound remarks, 112ff.

5. *The Simulacra*, 100. See also *The Crack in Space*, 114; *Galactic Pot-Healer*, 175–76; and "Piper in the Woods," S1, 158–59.

6. See Pierre-Henri Castel's remarks on the death drive as "what comes from the future," *Le Mal qui vient*, 101ff.

7. See Vladimir Safatle's article, "Para além da necropolítica.".

8. *Radio Free Albemuth*, 36. Compare *The World Jones Made*, 44–45, where Hitler is compared to a precog. Goebbels rightly said of Hitler that he lived in a "world of absolute fatality" (Heiber, *Hitler and His Generals*). Katherine Hayle shows how the Nazis are the very embodiment of regression in *The Man in the High Castle*, "Metaphysics and Metafiction in *The Man in the High Castle*," 60–61. [I was unable to locate the abovementioned Goebbels quotation in the English edition of Heiber's *Hitler and His Generals*. Lapoujade cites the French edition of the book (*Hitler parle à ses généraux* [Perrin, "Tempus," 2013], 324), as does Vladimir Safatle, referring to the same quotation, in the article cited in the note above. The English translation I use echoes the one used by Brian Massumi in his translation of Deleuze and Guattari's *A Thousand Plateaus* (see chapter 9, n. 32)—TN]

9. As his doctor tells him: "They've always classed paranoia as a mental illness. But it isn't! There's no lack of contact with reality—on the contrary, the paranoid is *directly* related to reality. He's a perfect empiricist. Not cluttered with ethical and moral-cultural inhibitions. The paranoid sees things as they really are; he's actually the only sane man" (S3, 166). And the paranoid boy's response: "I've been reading *Mein Kampf* [. . .]. It shows me I'm not alone."

10. See "Speculative Illustrations: Eduardo Paolozzi in Conversation with J. G. Ballard," 37–38. [Lapoujade cites the French translation of this conversation in Mavridorakis, *Art et science-fiction*, 85. His footnote continues: "The contributions to this volume insist on the Ballard/Smithson parallel, starting from the notion of entropy, which is present in the works of both artists."—TN]

11. Ballard, *The Crystal World*, 73. This analysis could be repeated for all of his early novels. Each dimension of time refers to a privileged material element: water for the past, sand (or dust) for the future, concrete for the present, and crystal for eternity. See David Pringle's essay, "The Fourfold Symbolism of J. G. Ballard." [Lapoujade cites the French translation of the essay in Mavridorakis, *Art et science-fiction*.—TN]

12. This aspect can also be found in Murakami, starting with *Hard-Boiled Wonderland and the End of the World*: parallel to the real world, there exists another world in which time is frozen and people, who are prisoners within a dying psychotic memory, explore a fabulous immemorial past. This *Spaltung* is the source of the fantastic in Murakami and can be found in most of his stories.

13. Ballard, *The Crystal World*, 93–94.

14. Robert Smithson, "A Tour of the Monuments of Passaic, New Jersey," 74. See also Smithson's essay "Entropy and the New Monuments." [Lapoujade cites French translations of both texts in Mavridorakis, *Art et science-fiction*, 213 and 179ff., respectively—TN]

6. THOSE WHO POSSESS WORLDS

1. "The World She Wanted," S2, 185: "I'm not sure Napoleon ever existed in my world [. . .]. I think he's just a name in the records, although some such person did exist in other worlds. In my world, Hitler was defeated; Roosevelt died—I'd be sorry about that, only I didn't know him, and he wasn't very real, anyway; they were both just images carried over from other people's worlds. . . ."

2. The drug plays nearly the same role as the sunglasses in the John Carpenter film *They Live* (1988). Ray Faraday Nelson, the author of the story that inspired the film ("Eight O'Clock in the Morning," published in 1963), was friends with Dick. Together they wrote the delirious novel *The Ganymede Takeover*, published in 1967.

3. Sutin, 92. Compare *Martian Time-Slip*, 82: "Purpose of life is unknown, and hence way to be is hidden from the eyes of living critters. Who can say if perhaps the schizophrenics are not correct? Mister, they take a brave journey."

4. See the story, "The Little Black Box" (S5) and *Do Androids Dream of Electric Sheep?*

5. *Exegesis*, 490. See also 606: "Everything is written down and has been written down from the beginning, as the Jews knew from the disclosure of the Torah. Basically, sacred history exists as information; first in terms of temporal sequence; first in order of ontology. *The mythic ritual is an entry key into the sacred narrative*. It functions the way an entry key of a computer functions vis-à-vis a given program."

6. "The Exit Door Leads In," S5, 387.

7. "You know there hasn't been any privacy for anybody for the last fifty years [. . .]. You work for an intelligence agency; don't kid me" (*Clans of the Alphane Moon*, 72).

8. "The Android and the Human," 198.

9. As Wiener explains: "When I compare the living organism with such a

machine, I do not for a moment mean that the specific physical, chemical, and spiritual processes of life as we ordinarily know it are the same as those of life-imitating machines. I mean simply that they both can exemplify locally anti-entropic processes" (*The Human Use of Human Beings*, 47).

10. Wiener, 49.

11. Wiener, 66: "We have modified our environment so radically that we must now modify ourselves in order to exist in this new environment." From this perspective, cybernetics is the privileged tool of the imperative to adapt that Barbara Stiegler describes in *Adapt!*.

12. Wiener, *Human Use of Human Beings*, 26–27: "Information is a name for the content of what is exchanged with the outer world as we adjust to it, and make our adjustment felt upon it."

13. [It appears that this quotation from Philip K. Dick has never been published in English. Lapoujade cites a volume of French translations—*Nouvelles, 1953–1963*, edited by Hélène Collon and published by Denoël (1997)—in which the quotation was included as an introductory note preceding the story "Service Call." Prior to that, the quotation appeared as a note preceding the same story in another French edition of Dick's stories: *Dédales Démesurés*, edited by Alain Dorémieux and published by Casterman (1982). It seems likely that Dick wrote this story note for *The Golden Man*, a 1980 collection of his stories, in which "Service Call" was not ultimately included. Of the eight stories in *Dédales Démesurés*, five were included in *The Golden Man*, and the notes for each of those were reproduced in French translation; the notes for the remaining three stories (including "Service Call") appear to have been published there (in French translation) for the first time. This is therefore my own translation of the French translation of Dick's story note. Many thanks to Hélène Collon, Frank Hollander, and Gilles Goullet, who provided invaluable assistance as I searched for this quotation.—TN]

14. In *VALIS*, Dick points out that California moves on from being interested in drugs to being interested in religion: "By now the epoch of drug-taking had

ended, and everyone had begun casting about for a new obsession. For us the new obsession, thanks to Fat, was theology" (195).

15. See Foucault, *Psychiatric Power*, 189.

16. See Deleuze, *Negotiations*, 174: "We're moving toward control societies that no longer operate by confining people but through continuous control and instant communication."

17. "The Android and the Human," 196.

7. ARTIFICIAL WORLDS

1. "This theme of faked memories is a constant thread in my writing over the years" ("If You Find This World Bad . . . ," 248).

2. *A Scanner Darkly*, 867. On the artificial character of California, see, for example, Mike Davis's portrait of Los Angeles in *City of Quartz*. On the way in which the "fake" is already developed in the amusement parks of Coney Island at the turn of the twentieth century, see Rem Koolhaas, *Delirious New York*.

3. Sutin, 200. Dick is referring to the laudatory article that Stanisław Lem devoted to him, which otherwise painted an unsparing portrait of American SF. See Lem, "Philip K. Dick: A Visionary among the Charlatans."

4. See Mattia Petricola's article, "Idéologie et ontologie des lieux de vie dans *Ubik* de Philip K. Dick." On Ballard, see Mavridorakis, *Art et science-fiction: la "Ballard Connection."*

5. See Petricola, "Idéologie et ontologie des lieux de vie dans *Ubik* de Philip K. Dick."

6. See Warhol's declaration in Foster, *The First Pop Age*, 110: "I don't want it to be essentially the same—I want it to be exactly the same. Because the more you look at the same exact thing, the more the meaning goes away, and the better and emptier you feel." And Roy Lichtenstein's, in the same book (275–76): "I don't draw a picture in order to reproduce it—I do it in order to recompose it. Nor am I trying to change it as much as possible. I try to make the minimum amount of change."

7. See Thierry de Duve, "Performance Here and Now: Minimal Art, a Plea for a New Genre of Theatre," and Georges Didi-Huberman, *Ce que nous voyons, ce qui nous regarde*.

8. See Robert Indiana's account in Victor Bockris, *The Life and Death of Andy Warhol*, 150, and the photographs of the exhibition at the Stable Gallery in New York in Claude Gintz, ed., *Regards sur l'art américain des années soixante*, 81.

9. This duality continues, in its own way, the avant-garde/kitsch polarity that Clement Greenberg developed in *Art and Culture*, tracing a series of marked oppositions: essence/appearance, rarefaction/saturation, seriousness/irony, true/false.

10. *The Simulacra*, 41 and also 101. See also *The Zap Gun*, 74, and *Galactic Pot-Healer*, 129–30.

11. "How to Build a Universe . . . ," 262. See also *A Scanner Darkly*, in which Los Angeles is described as "a fun park for grown-up kids" (867).

12. See also "Stability" (S1), "The Crystal Crypt" (S1), and "The Trouble with Bubbles" (S2).]

13. *The Man Who Japed*, 99. This method—which reappears several times throughout Dick's works—is not so far from the procedure Foucault describes in *Psychiatric Power* (129ff), when alienists would manipulate reality to make it conform to their patients' deliria.

14. This novel is one of the main sources of inspiration for Peter Weir's film *The Truman Show* (1998).

15. *The Divine Invasion*, 543.

16. Jameson, *Archaeologies of the Future*, 286–87: "For the apparent realism, or representationality, of SF has concealed another, far more complex temporal structure: not to give us 'images of the future [. . .] but rather to defamiliarize and restructure our experience of our own *present*."

17. See the discussion of the impossibility of distinguishing originals and copies in *The Man in the High Castle*, 55f.

18. [See ch. 6, n. 15.—TN]

19. *A Maze of Death*, 90: "As if all this, and ourselves, and the settlement— all are contained in a geodetic dome."

20. On the closed system of information, see Gregory Bateson's discussions of redundancy as a mode of duplication and the propagation of information. Cf. *Steps to an Ecology of Mind*, 406–7.

21. See also the story "The Defenders."

22. "How to Build a Universe . . . ," 261–62.

23. In *Lies, Inc.*, the model of the camp that Dick used was the Soviet work camp (173), but his descriptions still hold for many contemporary forms. On the contemporary politics of camps, see Michel Agier, ed., *Un monde de camps*.

8. THE DIGITAL HUMAN
(OR, WHAT IS AN ANDROID?)

1. "How to Build a Universe . . . ," 263.

2. This story (written in 1953, published in 1954) closely resembles the opening scenes of Don Siegel's film, *Invasion of the Body Snatchers* (1956), which is adapted from Jack Finney's novel, *The Body Snatchers*, published in 1955. Without a doubt, Dick, like Finney, was inspired by Robert A. Heinlein's 1951 novel, *The Puppet Masters*, in which aliens take control of human brains in order to make them their "marionettes." See also "The Hanging Stranger" (S3).

3. See the parody of this theme in the story "The War with the Fnools" (S5), in which the aliens, the Fnools, who have attempted to invade Earth in the guise of gas-station attendants, and then as folk dancers, now return as real estate agents.

4. Robinson, *The Novels of Philip K. Dick*, 29: "Definitions of humanity become more and more difficult, until in *Do Androids Dream of Electric Sheep?*

it takes a complex psychological test to determine who is human and who is machine." See also "Man, Android, and Machine," 211f.

5. *Galactic Pot-Healer*, 19. See, in particular, the story "The Exit Door Leads In" (S5).

6. Only rarely do machines take power in Dick's stories. Examples where they do can be found in the stories "James P. Crow" and "Autofac" (S2 and S4, respectively).

7. See Dick's 1976 recollection about the publication of "Service Call," quoted in S4, 464. On the importance of services in a capitalism of overproduction, see Deleuze, *Negotiations*, 181: "[Capitalism] no longer buys raw materials and no longer sells finished products: it buys finished products or assembles them from parts. What it seeks to sell is services, and what it seeks to buy, activities."

8. Compare the psyrobot of "Oh, to Be a Blobel!": "He put a twenty-dollar platinum coin into the slot and the analyst, after a pause, lit up. Its eyes shone with sociability and it swiveled about in its chair" (S4, 443).

9. Grégoire Chamayou, *A Theory of the Drone*, 207, and the entirety of chapter 23, "The Fabrication of Political Automata." Chamayou's remark takes as its starting point a text from Adorno's *Minima Moralia* on "robot-bombs" (the V-1 and V-2 missiles used by the Nazis) and focuses above all on the robotization and so-called humanization of lethal acts.

10. See Chamayou, 211: "This is a typical way of *fabricating irresponsibility*."

11. See "Second Variety" (adapted into the film *Screamers* in 1995 by Christian Duguay). On the human–machine substitution, see also the story "Nanny" (S1), which describes the confrontation between more and more perfected models of robot babysitters.

12. *We Can Build You*, 190: "Grief, emotional empathy, were written on his face. He fully felt the sorrows of the war, every single death."

13. See *The Dark-Haired Girl* and his portrait of her in *We Can Build You*: "Pris is wild, I thought. Not a part of us. Outside somewhere. Pris is pristine and in an awful way: all that goes on among and between people, all that we have here, fails to touch her" (210).

14. See the stories "Human Is" (S2) and "Progeny." In the latter, children are raised by robots and become completely inhuman: "And there could be no *Oedipus Complex*, with only robots around" (S2, 124).

15. Jameson, *Archaeologies of the Future*, 365, 366.

16. "The Little Black Box," S5, 9.

17. "How to Build a Universe . . .," 265.

18. William S. Burroughs, *Nova Express*, 48.

19. William S. Burroughs, *Naked Lunch*, 141.

20. Alfred Korzybski, "The Role of Language in the Perceptual Processes," 690: "If we "think" *verbally*, we act as biased observers and project onto the silent levels the structure of the language we use, so remaining in our rut of old orientations which make keen, unbiased observations ("perceptions"?) and creative work well-nigh impossible." Let us recall that Korzybski's theses became popular thanks, most notably, to A. E. van Vogt's novel, *The World of Null-A* ("null-A" designating non-Aristotelian logic).

21. See Jameson, *Archaeologies of the Future*, 288–89.

22. Wiener, *The Human Use of Human Beings*, 66.

23. "The Android and the Human," 191: "Becoming what I call, for lack of a better term, an android, means, as I said, to allow oneself to become a means, or to be pounded down, manipulated, made into a means without one's knowledge or consent—the results are the same. [. . .] Androidization requires obedience. And, most of all, *predictability*."

24. Simondon, *On the Mode of Existence of Technical Objects*, 16.

25. See Heims, *The Cybernetic Group*. From 1942 to 1953, the Macy Conferences brought together researchers from various disciplines in an attempt to establish a general science of the functioning of the mind. Notable partic-

ipants include Margaret Mead, Gregory Bateson, Norbert Wiener, John Von Neumann, Roman Jakobson, Claude Shannon, and many others. It is particularly worth noting the presence and interest of Harold Alexander Abramson, a doctor who worked for the CIA on a secret project focused on techniques of mental manipulation, especially as regards the effects of LSD on the mind (Project MK-Ultra).

26. In many respects, the distinction between analogical relations and digital relations closely matches the distinction that Bergson establishes in *Creative Evolution* between intuition and intelligence. On its own, intelligence thinks by means of the reconstruction of closed systems that are composed of discrete unities, based on the model of manufacture, while intuition proceeds by means of sympathy in relation to open, continuous, "musical" totalities, based on the model of creation.

27. "Philip K. Dick in Interview . . .," 40. [Lapoujade cites the French translation of this interview in Collon, *Regards sur Philip K. Dick.*—TN]

28. "Man, Android, and Machine," 223: "By more modern views we are overlapping fields, all of us, animals included, plants included. This is the ecosphere, and we are all in it. But what we don't realize is that the billions of discrete and entirely ego-oriented left-hemisphere brains have far less to say about the ultimate disposition of the world than does the collective noospheric Mind that comprises all our right brains and in which each of us shares. *It* will decide, and I do not think it impossible that this vast plasmic noosphere, considering that it covers our entire planet in a veil or layer, may interact outward into solar-energy fields and from there into cosmic fields."

29. Burroughs, *Naked Lunch*, 112.

30. *Radio Free Albemuth*, 187: "I had to become consciously aware—in a manner I could never forget—of what could be done with subliminal cueing in popular music."

31. See "The Little Black Box," S5, 29: "Telepathic power and empathy are two versions of the same thing." On the other hand, Dick can have one of the

characters in *The Ganymede Takeover* say: "You're a telepath; you read men's minds. But you don't understand them" (72). See also *The Game-Players of Titan*, 60.

32. "[In *Flow My Tears, the Policeman Said*] I am saying, 'In answer to the question, 'What is real?' the answer is: this kind of overpowering love,'" Sutin, 165. See *Flow My Tears, the Policeman Said*, 782: "Haven't you ever loved a child? It hurts your heart, the innermost part of you, where you can easily die."

33. *Exegesis*, 619: "USA 1974 is really Rome c. 45 C.E. Christ is really here; so is the kingdom. I found my way into it once. The long path is the short path—ponderous books of philosophy won't help me; Burroughs's *Junky* will."

34. *Radio Free Albemuth*, 109; and 150: "The U.S. and the U.S.S.R., I understood, were the two portions of the Empire as divided up by the Emperor Diocletian for purely administrative purposes; at heart it was a single entity, with a single value system. And its value system was the concept of the supremacy of the state."

35. See *VALIS*, Appendix, 386f.

36. Didi-Huberman, *Confronting Images*, 22.

37. *Exegesis*, 582: "So to explain 2-3-74 I draw on *The Tibetan Book of the Dead*, Orphism, Gnosticism, Neoplatonism, Buddhism, esoteric Christianity and the Kabbala." Allegro's thesis is returned to in *The Transmigration of Timothy Archer*, 684.

38. Sutin, 221. Thorazine is a medication used to treat acute psychosis.

39. See Maleval, *Logique du délire*, chapter II.

40. Sass, *The Paradoxes of Delusion*, 24: "It has not in fact been sufficiently noted how often schizophrenic delusions involve not belief in the unreal but disbelief in something that most people take to be true."

41. [Here, Lapoujade is using the term "arrière-monde," which is the standard French translation of Nietzsche's "Hinterwelt." This is Nietzsche's term of condemnation for any transcendent "true" reality, whether metaphysical (the Platonic Forms) or religious (Christian salvation), which could only ever

be approximated in life—and could therefore only ever be attained outside of, beyond, or *behind* (hinter/arrière) this world. I have opted to use "after-world," which is how Walter Kaufmann, R. J. Hollingdale, and Michael Hulse all translate the term in their versions of *Thus Spoke Zarathustra.*—TN]

9. HUNTING AND PARANOIA

1. D. H. Lawrence, *The Collected Letters of D. H. Lawrence*, 2:721–22.

2. On the over-valent idea, see. *The Transmigration of Timothy Archer*, 696–97.

3. Deleuze and Guattari, *Anti-Oedipus*, 254: "I too am a slave—these are the new words spoken by the master."

4. "The Android and the Human," 191.

5. See *Lies, Inc.*, in which a character breaks open a soldier's face like a shell and discovers an "inner face," a "wet, limp face, made of the sea, dripping, and at the same time stinking," which "possessed a single multi-lensed eye" (82).

6. See Ewen, *Captains of Consciousness*, especially chapter 3.

7. See the detailed portrait of the paranoid boss in *Clans of the Alphane Moon*, 96ff.

8. "The H-bomb was a monstrous, paranoid-logic error. The product of a paranoid nut," *The Zap Gun*, 77.

9. "Shell Game," S3, 234.

10. See "The Android and the Human," 208: "[. . .] because to the paranoid, nothing is a surprise; everything happens exactly as he expected, and sometimes even more so. It all fits into his system. For us, though, there can be no system; maybe *all* systems—that is, any theoretical, verbal, symbolic, semantic, etc., formulation that attempts to act as an all-encompassing, all-explaining hypothesis of what the universe is about—are manifestations of paranoia."

11. See the declaration of a character in the story "Null-O," S3, 166: "They've always classed paranoia as a mental illness. But it isn't! There's no lack of

contact with reality—on the contrary, the paranoid [. . .] sees things as they really are; he's actually the only sane man."

12. Herman Melville, *The Confidence-Man*, 212: the portrait of a man who ruminates on his hatred of Native Americans, to the point where "the thought develops such attraction, that much as straggling vapors troop from all sides to a storm-cloud, so straggling thoughts of other outrages troop to the nucleus thought, assimilate with it, and swell it. At last, taking counsel with the elements, he comes to his resolution. An intenser Hannibal, he makes a vow, the hate of which is a vortex from whose suction scarce the remotest chip of the guilty race may reasonably feel secure."

13. "The ultimate in paranoia is not when everyone is against you but when every*thing* is against you. Instead of 'My boss is plotting against me,' it would be 'My boss's phone is plotting against me,'" Sutin, 74–75. Compare the story "Colony" (S1), in which the characters disembark onto a hospitable planet, but are suddenly assaulted by their microscopes and bath towels.

14. Rogin, "Political Repression in the United States," 68: "In the first moment whites were pitted against peoples of color. In the second Americans were pitted against aliens. In the third, which revolves around mass society and the state, a national-security bureaucracy confronts the invisible agents of a foreign power."

10. BETWEEN LIFE AND DEATH

1. *A Scanner Darkly*, 1089: "The dead [. . .] who can still see, even if they can't understand: they are our camera."

2. See, for example, the young woman at the end of *The Transmigration of Timothy Archer*, 785: "I am a machine now. [. . .] A machine doesn't know any better; it simply grinds along, and maybe whirrs. [. . .] [It] keeps up its routine. It lives out what it supposes to be life: it maintains its schedule and obeys the laws. It does not drive its car over the speed limit on the Richardson Bridge."

3. *Ubik*, 746. On this point, see Serge Leclaire, "Jerome, or Death in the Life of the Obsessional."

4. *Dr. Bloodmoney*, 378: "That Bill-thing with Edie Keller lives somehow with the dead, Hoppy said to himself. Half in our world, half in the other."

5. Poe, "The Facts in the Case of M. Valdemar," 101. See the remarks from Roland Barthes, who sees this statement as "the invention of an unheard-of category: the *true-false*, the *yes-no*; the *death-life* is conceived as an incombinable, non-dialectic *whole*," *The Semiotic Challenge*, 286–87.

6. The novel presents him as a "mixture of Lincoln and Mussolini" (516) and a Christ-like figure (see Sutin, 302).

7. See Ernst H. Kantorowicz, *The King's Two Bodies*, especially 42ff.

8. *The Simulacra*, 160: "I'm Kate Rupert, the fourth one to take her place. I'm just an actress who looks enough like the original Nicole to be able to keep this job [. . .]. I have no real authority, in the ultimate sense. There's a council that governs." The figure of "Nicole" was inspired by Jackie Kennedy. See also "The Mold of Yancy" (S4), which describes the artificial construction of a reproducible popular character.

9. We should recall that, initially, avatars referred to incarnations in animal or human forms in Hinduism.

10. Rogin, "The King's Two Bodies: Lincoln, Wilson, Nixon, and Presidential Self-Sacrifice," 81ff.

11. The paranoid, fascist president in *Radio Free Albemuth* is directly inspired by Nixon, and the episode in which plumbers come in and install microphones and cameras in *A Scanner Darkly* (written in 1973 and revised in 1975) is a direct allusion to the Watergate scandal, which took place between 1972 and 1974.

11. BRICOLAGE (OR, THE RANDOM VARIABLE)

1. Henry James, "The Lesson of Balzac," 79ff.

2. See Lem, "Philip K. Dick: A Visionary among the Charlatans," 112.

3. See "Survey Team" and "The Crawlers," S3, 201. See also the story of the boy who is an outcast at school because he is the only one whose family does not have an atomic bomb shelter, "Foster, You're Dead!" (S3).

4. Jameson, *Archaeology of the Future*, 350. Jameson offers a thorough structural analysis of *Dr. Bloodmoney* in chapter 9 of the book: see "After Armageddon: Character Systems in *Dr. Bloodmoney*," (349–62).

5. At least four of Verne's stories belong to the "robinsonade" genre. Besides *Godfrey Morgan* and *The Mysterious Island*, there are also *Two Years' Vacation* and *The Castaways of the Flag*, the latter being presented as the sequel to Johann Davis Wyss' *The Swiss Family Robinson*.

6. See Dick's very instructive letter to Ron Goulart in which he explains how he constructs his novels, quoted in Sutin, 136–39.

7. This declaration is from one of the characters in *Dr. Bloodmoney*, 314–15. Conversely, this is the declaration of the person in charge of a commercial enterprise in *Martian Time-Slip*: "I am goddamn tired of being Norbert Steiner [. . .] I'm not good with my hands, I can't fix or make anything" (42–43).

8. Lévi-Strauss, *Wild Thought*, 21.

9. See equally Simondon, *On the Mode of Existence of Technical Objects*, where, in distinction to a conceptual or "major" symbolic knowledge, he describes a "minor" technical knowledge, belonging to the individual "endowed with a power of intuition and complicity with the world that will give him a very remarkable aptitude that can only manifest itself in work and not in consciousness or discourse" (106).

10. This early novella is heavily inspired by Dick's reading of Alfred Korzybski, whom he had discovered through A. E. van Vogt, one of the authors who had most inspired him when he was starting out.

11. Leo Steinberg, *Other Criteria*, 77–78, and 79: "It is probably no chance coincidence that the descriptive terms which have dominated American formalist criticism these past fifty years run parallel to the contemporaneous evolution of the Detroit automobile. [. . .] What I am saying here relates less to the pictures themselves than to the critical apparatus that deals with them."

12. Steinberg, 84.

13. Steinberg, 88: "And it seemed at times that Rauschenberg's work surface stood for the mind itself—dump, reservoir, switching center, abundant with concrete references freely associated."

14. See also his story about the rebirth of artisanal crafts, "Pay for the Printer" (S3).

15. "The Android and the Human," 194–95.

16. "The Variable Man," S1, 230. And *The Game-Players of Titan*, 171: "Mary is a variable and can't be previewed within causal frameworks; she introduces the acausal principle of synchronicity."

17. From a 1970 letter from Philip K. Dick to *SF Commentary*, quoted in "Caught in the Movement of a Hand-Wound Universe," Roger Zelazny's introduction to Gregg Rickman's *Philip K. Dick: In His Own Words*, xii-xiii. [Lapoujade cites an excerpt of this letter published in Collon, *Regards sur Philip K. Dick*.—TN] See the reflections of two small-time businessmen while a civil war is breaking out at the end of *The Simulacra*, 203: "It's good to be small [. . .] in times like these. And the smaller the better." And the praise for the plumber in *Radio Free Albemuth*, 270ff.

18. See William James, "Letter to Mrs. Henry Whitman, June 7, 1899," 90.

19. "The Android and the Human," 191.

20. "The Android and the Human," 205 (emphasis added).

21. Lévi-Strauss, *Wild Thought*, 20.

22. See, in particular, the role played by John W. Campbell, who, after having been an SF author, became the principal editor of SF stories for the magazine *Astounding Stories*, which he directed from the end of the 1930s until

his death in 1971. At the time when Dick began composing his first SF texts, the general rules—all of which he had to transgress—were the following: the events should be explained rationally; there should be a happy ending; the aliens should never be as good or as intelligent as the humans; individual or collective merit should always be valorized. On this point, see Robinson, *The Novels of Philip K. Dick*, ix ff.

23. Recall Lévi-Strauss's citation of Franz Boas, which is close to the conception of worlds in Dick; see *Wild Thought*, 24: "it would seem that mythological worlds have been built up, only to be shattered again, and that new worlds were built from the fragments."

24. Sutin, 154–55 and *Exegesis*, 512: "I don't write beautifully—I just write reports about our condition to go to those outside of cold-pak. I am an analyzer."

25. Sutin, 256.

26. See Jean Oury, *Création et schizophrénie*, 169–73.

27. *Exegesis*, 494.

28. *Radio Free Albemuth*, 180, and *Exegesis*, 537: "I am slowly being overwhelmed with wild surmise."

BIBLIOGRAPHY

BY PHILIP K. DICK

NOVELS

Four Novels of the 1960s, ed. Jonathan Lethem. New York: The Library of America, 2007.

- ► *The Man in the High Castle*
- ► *The Three Stigmata of Palmer Eldritch*
- ► *Do Androids Dream of Electric Sheep?*
- ► *Ubik*

Five Novels of the 1960s & 70s, ed. Jonathan Lethem. New York: The Library of America, 2008.

- ► *Martian Time-Slip*
- ► *Dr. Bloodmoney, or How We Got Along after the Bomb*
- ► *Now Wait for Last Year*
- ► *Flow My Tears, the Policeman Said*
- ► *A Scanner Darkly*

VALIS and Later Novels, ed. Jonathan Lethem. New York: The Library of America, 2009.

- ► *A Maze of Death*
- ► *VALIS*
- ► *The Divine Invasion*
- ► *The Transmigration of Timothy Archer*

Clans of the Alphane Moon. New York: Vintage Books, 2002.

Counter-Clock World. Boston: Mariner Books, 2012.

The Crack in Space. New York: Vintage Books, 2005.

The Dark-Haired Girl, ed. Paul Williams. Willimantic, Conn.: Mark V. Ziesing, 1988.

Eye in the Sky. New York: Vintage Books, 2003.

Galactic Pot-Healer. Boston: Mariner Books, 2013.

The Game-Players of Titan. Boston: Mariner Books, 2012.

The Ganymede Takeover (with Ray Nelson). New York: Ace Books, 1967.

Lies, Inc. New York: Vintage Books, 2004.

The Man Who Japed. New York: Vintage Books, 2002.

Nick and the Glimmung. London: Victor Gollancz, 1988.

Our Friends from Frolix 8. New York: Vintage Books, 2003.

The Penultimate Truth. New York: Vintage Books, 2004.

Radio Free Albemuth. Boston: Mariner Books, 2020.

The Simulacra. New York: Vintage Books, 2002.

Solar Lottery. New York: Vintage Books, 2003.

Time Out of Joint. Boston: Mariner Books, 2012.

We Can Build You. Boston: Mariner Books, 2012.

The World Jones Made. New York: Vintage Books, 1993.

The Zap Gun. New York: Vintage Books, 2002.

STORIES

The Complete Stories of Philip K. Dick, Vol. 1: The King of the Elves (1947–1952). Burton, Mich.: Subterranean Press, 2010 [S1].

The Complete Stories of Philip K. Dick, Vol. 2: Adjustment Team (1952–1953). Burton, Mich.: Subterranean Press, 2011 [S2].

The Complete Stories of Philip K. Dick, Vol. 3: Upon the Dull Earth (1953–1954). Burton, Mich.: Subterranean Press, 2012 [S3].

The Complete Stories of Philip K. Dick, Vol. 4: The Minority Report (1954–1963). Burton, Mich.: Subterranean Press, 2013 [S4].

The Complete Stories of Philip K. Dick, Vol. 5: We Can Remember It for You Wholesale (1963–1981). Burton, Mich.: Subterranean Press, 2014 [S5].

OTHER

The Exegesis of Philip K. Dick, ed. Pamela Jackson and Jonathan Lethem. Boston: Houghton Mifflin Harcourt, 2011.

The Shifting Realities of Philip K. Dick: Selected Literary and Philosophical Writings, ed. Lawrence Sutin. New York: Pantheon Books, 1995.

- ▸ "How to Build a Universe That Doesn't Fall Apart Two Days Later"
- ▸ "If You Find This World Bad, You Should See Some of the Others"
- ▸ "Introduction to *The Golden Man*"
- ▸ "The Android and the Human"

ON PHILIP K. DICK

Apel, D. Scott, ed. "Philip K. Dick in Interview with D. Scott Apel and Kevin C. Briggs." In *Philip K. Dick: The Dream Connection*. Boulder Creek, Calif.: Atomic Drop Press, 2014.

Collon, Hélène, ed. *Regards sur Philip K. Dick: Le Kalédickoscope*, 2d ed. Paris: Encrage / Belles Lettres, 2006.

Déléage, Pierre, and Emmanuel Grimaud. "Anomalie: Champ faible, niveau légumes," *Gradhiva*, no. 29. Paris: Musée du quai Branly, 2019.

Hayles, Katherine. "Metaphysics and Metafiction in *The Man in the High Castle*." In *Philip K. Dick*, eds. Martin Harry Greenberg and Joseph D. Olander. New York: Taplinger Publishing Company, 1983.

Lem, Stanisław. "Philip K. Dick: A Visionary among the Charlatans," trans. Robert Abernathy. In *Microworlds: Writings on Science Fiction and Fantasy*, ed. Franz Rottensteiner. San Diego: Harcourt Brace & Company, 1984.

Petricola, Mattia. "Idéologie et ontologie des lieux de vie dans *Ubik* de Philip K. Dick." In *Lieux de vie en science-fiction*, ed. Danièle André. Paris: Books on Demand, 2022.

Robinson, Kim Stanley. *The Novels of Philip K. Dick*. Ann Arbor, Mich.: UMI Research Press, 1984.

Spinrad, Norman. "The Transmogrification of Philip K. Dick." In *Science Fiction in the Real World*. Carbondale: Southern Illinois University Press, 1990.

Sutin, Lawrence. *Divine Invasions: A Life of Philip K. Dick*. New York: Harmony Books, 1989.

Wolk, Anthony. "The Swiss Connection." In *Philip K. Dick: Contemporary Critical Interpretations*, ed. Samuel J. Umland. Westport, Conn.: Greenwood Press, 1995.

Zelazny, Roger. "Caught in the Movement of a Hand-Wound Universe." In *Philip K. Dick: In His Own Words*, ed. Gregg Rickman, rev. ed. Long Beach, Calif.: Fragments West/The Valentine Press, 1988.

OTHER

Agier, Michel, ed. *Un monde de camps*. Paris: Éditions La Découverte, 2014.

Alferi, Pierre. *Des enfants et des monstres*. Paris: P.O.L., 2004.

Amis, Kingsley. *New Maps of Hell*. New York: Harcourt, Brace and Company, 1960.

Aristotle, *Topics*, trans. W. A. Pickard-Cambridge, in *The Complete Works of Aristotle*, vol. 1, ed. Jonathan Barnes, Bollingen Series 71. Princeton, N.J.: Princeton University Press, 1984.

Artaud, Antonin. "Umbilical Limbo." In *Collected Works of Antonin Artaud*, vol. 1, trans. Victor Corti. London: Calder & Boyars, 1968.

Artaud, Antonin. "Witchcraft and Cinema." In *Collected Works of Antonin Artaud*, vol. 3, trans. Alastair Hamilton. London: Calder & Boyars, 1972.

Artaud, Antonin. *La Coquille et le Clergyman*. In *Collected Works of Antonin Artaud*, vol. 3 trans. Alastair Hamilton. London: Calder & Boyars, 1972.

Balibar, Étienne. *Identity and Difference: John Locke and the Invention of Consciousness*, ed. Stella Sandford, trans. Warren Montag. London: Verso, 2013.

Ballard, J. G. "Speculative Illustrations: Eduardo Paolozzi in Conversation with J. G. Ballard." In *Extreme Metaphors: Selected Interviews with J. G. Ballard, 1967–2008*, ed. Simon Sellars and Dan O'Hara. London: Fourth Estate, 2012.

Ballard, J. G. *The Crystal World*. New York: Farrar, Straus & Giroux, 1966.

Barthes, Roland. *The Semiotic Challenge*, trans. Richard Howard. Berkeley: University of California Press, 1994.

Bateson, Gregory. *Steps to an Ecology of Mind*. New York: Ballantine Books, 1972.

Bergson, Henri. "Dreams." In *Mind-Energy*, trans. H. Wildon Carr. New York: Henry Holt and Company, 1920.

Binswanger, Ludwig. *Dream and Existence*, ed. Keith Hoeller. New Jersey: Humanities Press, 1993.

Binswanger, Ludwig. *Melancholie und Manie: Phänomenologische Studien*. Pfullingen: Verlag Günther Neske, 1960.

Binswanger, Ludwig. *Mélancolie et manie: Études phénoménologiques*, trans. Jean-Michel Azorin, Yves Totoyan, and Arthur Tatossian. Paris: PUF, 2002.

Binswanger, Ludwig. *The Case of Ellen West: An Anthropological-Clinical Study*, trans. Werner M. Mendel and Joseph Lyons. In *Existence: A New Dimension in Psychiatry and Psychology*, ed. Rollo May, Ernest Angel, and Henri F. Ellenberger. New York: Simon & Schuster, 1958.

Bockris, Victor. *The Life and Death of Andy Warhol*. New York: Bantam Books, 1989.

Burroughs, William S. *Nova Express*. New York: Grove Press, 1992.

Burroughs, William S. *Naked Lunch*. New York: Grove Press, 2001.

Castel, Pierre-Henri. *Le Mal qui vient*. Paris: Éditions du Cerf, 2018.

Chamayou, Grégoire. *A Theory of the Drone*, trans. Janet Lloyd. New York: The New Press, 2015.

Dadoun, Roger. "Les ombilics du rêve." *Nouvelle Revue de psychanalyse*, no. 5 (1973), "L'espace du rêve."

Davis, Mike, *City of Quartz: Excavating the Future in Los Angeles*. London: Verso, 2018.

de Duve, Thierry. "Performance Here and Now: Minimal Art, a Plea for a New Genre of Theatre," *Open Letter* (Special Issue: Essays on Performance and Cultural Politicization) no. 5–6 (Summer-Autumn 1983).

Deleuze, Gilles. *Negotiations: 1972–1990*, trans. Martin Joughin. New York: Columbia University Press, 1995.

Deleuze, Gilles, and Félix Guattari, *Anti-Oedipus: Capitalism and Schizophrenia*, trans. Robert Hurley, Mark Seem, and Helen R. Lane. Minneapolis: University of Minnesota Press, 1983.

Didi-Huberman, Georges. *Ce que nous voyons, ce qui nous regarde*. Paris: Les Éditions de Minuit, 1992.

Didi-Huberman, Georges. *Confronting Images: Questioning the Ends of a Certain History of Art*, trans. John Goodman. State College: Penn State University Press, 2004.

Ewen, Stuart. *Captains of Consciousness*. New York: Basic Books, 2001.

Foster, Hal. *The First Pop Age*. Princeton, N.J.: Princeton University Press, 2012.

Foucault, Michel. "Dream, Imagination and Existence," trans. Forrest Williams. In Binswanger, *Dream and Existence*.

Foucault, Michel. *Psychiatric Power: Lectures at the Collège de France, 1973–1974*, ed. Jacques Lagrange, trans. Graham Burchell. New York: Palgrave Macmillan, 2006.

Foucault, Michel. *The Order of Things: An Archaeology of the Human Sciences*, trans. Alan Sheridan. New York: Pantheon Books, 1970.

Freud, Sigmund. "Formulations Regarding the Two Principles in Mental Functioning," trans. M. N. Searl. In *General Psychological Theory: Papers on Metapsychology*. New York: Touchstone, 1991.

Freud, Sigmund. *The Interpretation of Dreams*, trans. James Strachey. New York: Basic Books, 1960.

Freud, Sigmund. *The Psychopathology of Everyday Life*, trans. A. A. Brill. New York: MacMillan, 1915.

Freud, Sigmund. *The Schreber Case*, trans. Andrew Webber. New York: Penguin Books, 2002.

Gintz, Claude, ed. *Regards sur l'art américain des années soixante*. Paris: Éditions Territoires, 1979.

Green, André. "De l'"Esquisse' à 'L'interprétation des rêves': coupure et clo-ture." In *Nouvelle Revue de psychanalyse*, no. 5 (Spring 1972).

Greenberg, Clement. *Art and Culture: Critical Essays*. Boston: Beacon Press, 1961.

Heiber, Helmut. *Hitler and His Generals: Military Conferences 1942–1945*, trans. Roland Winter, Krista Smith, and Mary Beth Friedrich. New York: Enigma Books, 2003.

Heims, Steve J. *The Cybernetic Group*. Cambridge, Mass.: MIT Press, 1991.

Husserl, Edmund. *Experience and Judgment: Investigations in a Genealogy of Logic*, trans. James S. Churchill and Karl Ameriks. Evanston, Ill.: North-western University Press, 1973.

James, Henry. "The Lesson of Balzac." In *The Question of Our Speech; The Lesson of Balzac: Two Lectures*. Boston: Houghton Mifflin Company, 1905.

James, William. *The Letters of William James*, vol. 2, ed. Henry James. Boston: The Atlantic Monthly Press, 1920.

Jameson, Fredric. *Archaeologies of the Future: The Desire Called Utopia and Other Science Fictions*. London: Verso, 2005.

Jung, C. G. "Foreword." In *The I Ching, or, Book of Changes*, the Richard Wilhelm translation from Chinese into German, rendered into English by Cary F.

Baynes, Bollingen Series 19. Princeton, N.J.: Princeton University Press, 1977.

Kahn, Charles H. *The Art and Thought of Heraclitus: An Edition of the Fragments with Translation and Commentary*. London: Cambridge University Press, 1979.

Kantorowicz, Ernst H. *The King's Two Bodies: A Study in Medieval Political Theology*. Princeton, N.J.: Princeton University Press, 2016.

Koolhaas, Rem. *Delirious New York: A Retroactive Manifesto for Manhattan*. New York: The Monacelli Press, 1994.

Korzybski, Alfred. "The Role of Language in the Perceptual Processes." In *Collected Writings: 1920–1950*, ed. M. Kendig. Englewood, N.J.: International Non-Aristotelian Library, Institute of General Semantics, 1990.

Laplanche, Jean. *Problématiques I*. Paris: PUF, 2006.

Laplanche, Jean, and Jean-Bertrand Pontalis. *The Language of Psycho-Analysis*, trans. Donald Nicholson-Smith. New York: W. W. Norton & Company, 1973.

Lapoujade, David. *The Lesser Existences: Étienne Souriau, an Aesthetics for the Virtual*, trans. Erik Beranek. Minneapolis: University of Minnesota Press, 2021.

Lapoujade, David. *Powers of Time: Versions of Bergson*, trans. Andrew Goffey. New York: University of Minnesota Press, 2018.

Lavocat, Françoise, ed. *La Théorie littéraire des mondes possible*. Paris: CNRS Éditions, 2010.

Lawrence, D. H. *The Collected Letters of D. H. Lawrence*, vol. 2, ed. Harry T. Moore. London: William Heinemann Ltd., 1962.

Lecercle, Jean-Jacques. *Philosophy through the Looking Glass: Language, Nonsense, Desire*. La Salle, Ill.: Open Court, 1985.

Leclaire, Serge. "Jerome, or Death in the Life of the Obsessional." In *Returning to Freud: Clinical Psychoanalysis in the School of Lacan*, ed. and trans. Stuart Schneiderman. New Haven, Conn.: Yale University Press, 1980.

Lévi-Strauss, Claude. *Wild Thought*, trans. Jeffrey Mehlman and John Leavitt. Chicago: University of Chicago Press, 2021.

Mack, John E. *Abduction: Human Encounters with Aliens*. New York: Ballantine Books, 1995.

Maleval, Jean-Claude. *Logique du délire*. Rennes: Presses Universitaires de Rennes, 2011.

Mavridorakis, Valérie, ed. *Art et science-fiction: la Ballard Connection*, Geneva: Musée d'Art Moderne et Contemporain (MAMCO), 2011.

Meillassoux, Quentin. *Science Fiction and Extro-Science Fiction*, trans. Alyosha Edlebi. Minneapolis: Univocal, 2015.

Melville, Herman. *The Confidence-Man: His Masquerade*, Champaign, Ill.: Dalkey Archive Press, 2007.

Merleau-Ponty, Maurice. *The Visible and the Invisible*, trans. Alphonso Lingis. Evanston, Ill.: Northwestern University Press, 1968.

Oury, Jean. *Création et schizophrénie*. Paris: Éditions Galilée, 1989.

Poe, Edgar Allan. "The Facts in the Case of M. Valdemar." In *The Complete Tales and Poems of Edgar Allan Poe*. New York: The Modern Library, 1938.

Pringle, David. "The Fourfold Symbolism of J. G. Ballard." In David Pringle, *Earth Is the Alien Planet: J. G. Ballard's Fourth Dimensional Nightmare*. San Bernardino, Calif.: Borgo Press, 1979.

Rogin, Michael Paul. "Political Repression in the United States." In *Ronald Reagan, the Movie, and Other Episodes in Political Demonology*. Berkeley: University of California Press, 1987.

Rogin, Michael Paul. "The King's Two Bodies: Lincoln, Wilson, Nixon, and Presidential Self-Sacrifice." In *Ronald Reagan, the Movie, and Other Episodes in Political Demonology*. Berkeley: University of California Press, 1987.

Safatle, Vladimir. "Para além da necropolítica." This essay was originally published online by N-1 Edições. It is now available online on the A Terra é Redonda website https://aterraeredonda.com.br/para-alem-da-necropo litica. An English translation was published in *Crisis and Critique 7*,

no. 3: https://www.crisiscritique.org/storage/app/media/2020-11-24/
vladimir-safatle.pdf.

Sartre, Jean-Paul. *The Imaginary: A Phenomenological Psychology of the Imagination*, trans. Jonathan Webber. London: Routledge, 2004.

Sass, Louis A. *The Paradoxes of Delusion: Wittgenstein, Schreber, and the
Schizophrenic Mind*. Ithaca, N.Y.: Cornell University Press, 1994.

Schmutz, Jacob. "Qui a inventé les mondes possibles?" In *Cahiers philoso-
phiques de l'université de Caen*, no 42 (2006).

Schütz, Alfred. "Don Quixote and the Problem of Reality." In *Collected Papers,
vol. II: Studies in Social Theory*, ed. Arvid Brodersen, Phaenomenologica,
vol. 15. Dordrecht: Springer, 1976.

Simondon, Gilbert. *Individuation in Light of Notions of Form and Information*,
vol. 1, trans. Taylor Adkins. Minneapolis: University of Minnesota Press,
2020.

Simondon, Gilbert. *On the Mode of Existence of Technical Objects*, trans. Cecile
Malaspina and John Rogove. Minneapolis: Univocal, 2016.

Smithson, Robert. "A Tour of the Monuments of Passaic, New Jersey." In *Robert
Smithson: The Collected Writings*, ed. Jack Flam. Berkeley: University of
California Press, 1996.

Steinberg, Leo. *Other Criteria: Confrontations with Twentieth-Century Art*. London: Oxford University Press, 1972.

Stiegler, Barbara. *Adapt! On a New Political Imperative*, trans. Adam Hocker.
New York: Fordham University Press, 2022.

Todorov, Tzvetan. *The Fantastic: A Structural Approach to a Literary Genre*,
trans. Richard Howard. Ithaca, N.Y.: Cornell University Press, 1975.

Watzlawick, Paul. *The Language of Change: Elements of Therapeutic Communication*. New York: Basic Books, 1978.

Wiener, Norbert. *The Human Use of Human Beings: Cybernetics and Society*.
New York: Avon Books, 1967.

David Lapoujade is professor of philosophy at Université Paris 1–Sorbonne, and author of numerous books, including *William James: Empiricism and Pragmatism*, *Aberrant Movements: The Philosophy of Gilles Deleuze*, *Powers of Time: Versions of Bergson* (Minnesota, 2017), and *The Lesser Existences: Étienne Souriau, An Aesthetics for the Virtual* (Minnesota, 2021).

Erik Beranek is a writer, editor, and translator based in Philadelphia. He has translated works by Jacques Rancière, Étienne Souriau, Michel Foucault, and David Lapoujade and is an editor at *Hopscotch Translation*.